THE HEART OF THE CROSS

THE
HEART
OF THE
CROSS

James Montgomery Boice

Philip Graham Ryken

CROSSWAY BOOKS • WHEATON, ILLINOIS
A DIVISION OF GOOD NEWS PUBLISHERS

The Heart of the Cross

Published by Crossway Books
A division of Good News Publishers
1300 Crescent Street
Wheaton, Illinois 60187

Design: Cindy Kiple

First printing, 1999

Printed in the United States of America

Library of Congress Cataloging-in-Publication Data
Boice, James Montgomery, 1938–
   The heart of the cross / James Montgomery Boice, Philip
Graham Ryken.
      p.   cm.
   Includes bibliographical references.
   ISBN 1-58134-039-7 (hardcover : alk. paper)
   1. Holy Cross. I. Ryken, Philip Graham, 1966–   . II. Title.
BT465.B65   1999
232.96—dc21   98-47905
                                                    CIP

15   14   13   12   11   10   09   08   07   06   05   04   03   02   01   00   99
15   14   13   12   11   10   9   8   7   6   5   4   3   2   1

Jesus didn't want to die, either.

He knew what was coming.

And he knew it wouldn't be fun.

So why did he go through with it?

Because to beat death,

somebody had to conquer it

once and for all.

CONTENTS

Preface   8

PART ONE: *Words from the Cross*

1. *The Heart of God* (Luke 23:34)   13
   by James Montgomery Boice

2. *The Luckiest Man Alive* (Luke 23:43)   21
   by Philip Graham Ryken

3. *Family Ties* (John 19:26-27)   29
   by Philip Graham Ryken

4. *Human After All* (John 19:28)   37
   by Philip Graham Ryken

5. *Forsaken, Yet Not Forsaken* (Matthew 27:46)   45
   by Philip Graham Ryken

6. *Mission Accomplished* (John 19:30)   53
   by Philip Graham Ryken

7. *Homeward Bound* (Luke 23:46)   61
   by James Montgomery Boice

PART TWO: *The Real Last Words of Christ*

8. *A Word for the Seeker* (John 20:15)   71
   by Philip Graham Ryken

9. *A Word for the Fearful* (Matthew 28:10)   79
   by Philip Graham Ryken

10. *A Word for the Restless* (John 20:19, 21)   87
    by Philip Graham Ryken

11. *A Word for the Troubled* (Luke 24:27)   95
    by James Montgomery Boice

12. *A Word for the Skeptical* (Luke 24:39)   103
    by Philip Ryken

13. *A Word for the Fallen* (John 21:17)   111
    by Philip Graham Ryken

14. *A Word for Everyone* (Matthew 28:18-20)   119
    by James Montgomery Boice

PART THREE: *The Message of the Cross*

15. *The Necessity of the Cross* (Acts 2:23)   129
    by Philip Graham Ryken

16. *The Offense of the Cross* (Hebrews 12:2)   137
    by Philip Graham Ryken

17. *The Peace of the Cross* (Colossians 1:20)   145
    by Philip Graham Ryken

18. *The Power of the Cross* (1 Corinthians 1:18)   153
    by Philip Graham Ryken

19. *The Triumph of the Cross* (Colossians 2:15)   161
    by Philip Graham Ryken

20. *The Boast of the Cross* (Galatians 6:14)   169
    by Philip Graham Ryken

21. *The Way of the Cross* (Luke 9:23)   177
    by James Montgomery Boice

Notes   185

PREFACE

t is impossible to overestimate the importance of the cross of Jesus Christ. For whether we are thinking about Christ's words from the cross, his words about the cross, or the biblical doctrines of the cross, in every case the cross is central to Christianity. Indeed, we are saying more. We are saying that without the cross there is no Christianity. By itself the Incarnation does not provide us with genuine Christianity. It merely gives us sentimental stories for Christmas. The example of Christ alone is not Christianity since no one is saved by imitating Jesus. Even the Resurrection alone is not the essence of biblical religion.

So I repeat, it is impossible to overestimate the importance of what Jesus accomplished for his people on the cross.

Two truths follow. On the one hand, if the cross of Christ is the very heart and essence of Christianity, we should expect that its meaning is simplicity itself. And it is. For example, "Christ died for our sins according to the Scriptures" (1 Cor. 15:3). What could be plainer than that? Or we read, "Believe in the Lord Jesus, and you will be saved" (Acts 16:31). The Bible often presents the cross that way—simply and with the most direct and pressing demand for faith.

On the other hand, if the cross is the very essence of Christianity, we might also expect it to stretch our minds to the utmost as we try to probe its depths. And we find that too. Indeed, we find that in some measure the full meaning of the cross is always well beyond our grasp. In this double sense, the doctrines of the cross might be described by the words one writer used to describe the theology of the fourth Gospel, the Gospel of John. He called it "a pool in which a child can wade" as well as "an ocean in which an elephant can swim."

How does one deal with a matter as central, simple, and yet as fully rich and inexhaustible as the cross? What my colleague Philip Ryken and I decided to do was to expound the Bible's teaching about the cross in three series of Lenten messages at Tenth Presbyterian Church in Philadelphia where we serve together as pastors. He has done the bulk of this Lenten preaching, handling sixteen of the following twenty-one studies. But I have had the privilege of sharing with him by handling the others. I have been blessed by his preaching, as I trust he has with mine. Together both of us pray that you will be blessed as you reflect with us on the meaning and application of these important Bible texts.

Apart from the cross the Christian religion becomes only a type of human self-deification that leads to arrogance and presumption, a religion that supposes wrongly that we can somehow save ourselves. With the cross at the center, Christianity offers the sole ground for our standing before God as justified men and women and the only adequate motivation for a life of rest in God and genuine self-sacrifice for others. We are led to give all we have because on the cross Jesus gave all he had for us.

> *Were the whole realm of nature mine,*
> *That were a present far too small;*
> *Love so amazing, so divine,*
> *Demands my soul, my life, my all.*

Isaac Watts wrote those words in 1701, and he was right. I trust you will discover this truth in new ways as you read, think about, and pray over these important Bible passages with us.

JAMES MONTGOMERY BOICE
PHILADELPHIA, PENNSYLVANIA

PART ONE

WORDS

FROM THE

CROSS

"*Father,*

forgive them,

for they do not

know what

they are doing."

LUKE 23:34

1

The Heart of God

James Montgomery Boice

here is something significant about the last words of men and women because when a person comes face to face with death, what he or she is often rises to the surface. Napoleon Bonaparte (1769-1821), the French general and emperor, said, "I die before my time, and my body will be given back to the earth. Such is the fate of him who has been called the great Napoleon. What an abyss between my deep misery and the eternal kingdom of Christ."

Voltaire (1694-1778), the famous French infidel, is reported to have said to his doctor, "I am abandoned by God and man! I will give you half of what I am worth if you will give me six months' life."

Thomas Hobbes (1588-1679), the brilliant skeptic who corrupted the faith of some of England's great men, exclaimed, "If I had the whole world, I would give it to live one day. I shall be glad to find a hole to creep out of the world at. I am about to take a leap into the dark."

FAMOUS "LAST WORDS"

I have always thought it unfortunate that the seven sayings of Jesus on the cross have been called his "last words," because the perhaps unwitting implication is that Jesus did not rise again and therefore never said

13

anything else. Jesus did rise again, of course. The existence of Christianity is one of the best proofs of that astonishing fact. And Jesus had more to say, even before he returned to heaven forty days after returning to life. Those words are the true "last words," if any are.

On the other hand, the sayings from the cross, although wrongly called Jesus' last words, are significant, for several reasons. (1) They show that Jesus was in clear possession of his faculties until the very last moment, when he delivered up his spirit to God. (2) They show that he understood his death to be an atonement for the sin of the world. And (3) they show that he knew his death would be effective in doing that. He was satisfied with what he was doing, and he did not die in despair. Moreover, the words also exhibit his well-known concern and love for other persons, even at the moment of his most acute suffering.

Jesus' words from the cross are these:

1. "Father, forgive them, for they do not know what they are doing" (Luke 23:34). These words are a prayer for God to forgive those who were crucifying him. They show the merciful heart of the Savior.

2. "I tell you the truth, today you will be with me in paradise" (Luke 23:43). These words were spoken to the believing thief and were a confident promise of salvation. They show that while life lasts, it is never too late to believe on Jesus and be saved.

3. "Dear woman, here is your son" and "Here is your mother" (John 19:26-27). Here Jesus commended his mother, Mary, to the care of John, one of his disciples. It shows Jesus' concern for family ties.

4. "I am thirsty" (John 19:28). This request shows the true humanity of Jesus. But it also shows his concern that every facet of his death be in accord with the Bible's prophecies about him.

5. "My God, my God, why have you forsaken me?" (Mark 15:34; Matt. 27:46). This statement is the most shattering of all. It reveals

more than any other what was really happening on the cross. It teaches the nature of the atonement and what our salvation cost God.

6. "It is finished" (John 19:30). These are the most important words, because they refer not to Jesus' life, as if he were saying, "It is over," but to his atonement for sin. It is because Jesus made a complete and final atonement for sin that we can be sure of our salvation.

7. "Father, into your hands I commit my spirit" (Luke 23:46). These words show Jesus to have been in control of his life until the very end. They also show that the relationship between himself and the Father, which earlier had in some sense been broken, was now restored.

These sayings have fascinated preachers and laymen for two thousand years. They have been interpreted as teaching seven duties: 1) to forgive our enemies, 2) to have faith in Christ, 3) to honor our parents, 4) to set the highest possible value on the fulfillment of God's Word, 5) to cling to God even in life's darkest moments, 6) to persevere at whatever task God has given us to the very end, and 7) to yield all things, even life itself, to God at God's bidding.

Yet, far more important than looking at these words to learn our duties is to look at them for what they teach us about the nature and work of Christ himself, which is how we are looking at them in this book. They teach that Jesus died to save us from our sin; that is what his coming to earth was all about. They teach that as long as we are alive, it is never too late to turn from our sin and trust in Jesus as our Savior. The dying thief did that, and he was told by Jesus, "Today you will be with me in paradise" (Luke 23:43). It is our most important wish that as a result of this book, some might pass from spiritual death to spiritual life, as that man did.

A GREAT FORGIVENESS

We start with the first of these "last" sayings: "Father, forgive them, for they do not know what they are doing" (Luke 23:34). These words were spoken in the first moments of the crucifixion when Jesus, along with the two criminals who were executed with him, was stretched out on the rough timbers and felt excruciating pain as the thick iron nails were driven through the bones of his wrists and feet and the cumbersome cross was hoisted upward and allowed to fall down suddenly into the hole prepared for it. Death by crucifixion was probably the most cruel and lingering mode of execution ever devised by human beings.

But the crucifixion of Jesus was not only *cruel*. In his case it was also *unjust*, because he was innocent of any crime. That very morning the judge in his trial, Pontius Pilate, had declared him innocent—not only once but three times: "I find no basis for a charge against him" (John 18:38; 19:4, 6). Pilate had consented to the crucifixion only because Jesus' enemies had threatened to send a report to Caesar saying that Pilate was harboring a dangerous insurrectionist, a person who made himself out to be a king. That is why Pilate attached his written notice to the cross: "This is the King of the Jews." He didn't want anyone to be able to say that he was soft on political pretenders.

Not only was the crucifixion cruel and unjust. It was a *disgrace* and a *humiliation* too. Cicero, the famous orator, said rightly, although with an exalted sense of Roman dignity and ethnic pride, "To bind a Roman citizen is a crime, to flog him is an abomination, to slay him almost an act of murder: to crucify him is—what? There is no word that can possibly describe so horrible a deed."[1]

Here is the situation. Jesus was cruelly, unjustly, and disgracefully executed. Yet in the very moment of his most acute suffering he prayed for forgiveness for his enemies: "Father, forgive them, for they do not know what they are doing."

Did God hear that prayer? Of course, though we will never know the full extent of God's answer until we get to heaven and find out how many who were involved in that unjust trial and crucifixion later repented of their sin and came to believe on Jesus as their Savior.

John Charles Ryle, a great Anglican bishop of the last century, wrote: "We have probably not the least idea how many of the conversions to God at Jerusalem which took place during the first six months after the crucifixion, were the direct reply to this marvelous prayer. Perhaps this prayer was the first step towards the penitent thief's repentance. Perhaps it was one means of affecting the centurion, who declared our Lord 'a righteous man,' and the people who 'smote their breasts and returned.' Perhaps the three thousand converted on the day of Pentecost, foremost, it may be at one time among our Lord's murderers, owed their conversion to this very prayer. . . . We may be sure that this wondrous prayer was heard."[2]

Many people have been converted by this prayer since that time too as it has been explained in scores of preaching services. It teaches that Jesus is amazingly compassionate, inexplicably gracious. There is no one on earth, either now or at any other time, who is too far gone in sin or too hard of heart for him to care for. He cares for you and offers you forgiveness for your sin, if you will have it. If you are seeking any encouragement to repent and believe on Christ, this prayer provides it.

FORGIVENESS AT A GREAT COST

There is something else we should understand about this first saying of Jesus from the cross, and it is this: Not only was this a prayer for forgiveness and a great forgiveness at that—it was also a forgiveness prayed for at an enormous cost. This is because forgiveness does not come cheap. And the reason it does not come cheap is because God is God, the holy and just ruler of the universe, and a just God must act justly. Even God, especially God, must do what is right.

What is right? The right thing is that sin should be punished, evil must be judged. What we should expect if God were to act justly in this situation and do nothing else is that Pilate who judged, the soldiers who killed, the leaders who plotted, and the people who cried out for Jesus' death should have been punished. Because their sin was the great one of murdering the only beloved Son of God, they should have been punished for their sins in hell.

We can understand how God might want to forgive at no cost. We would like to do that too. Who does not want to be forgiving? But how can a just God both forgive and be just at the same time? The answer is the cross. And it is why these particular words were spoken from the cross and not before or in some other situation. It is because Jesus was taking the place of sinners in his death, taking your place and mine, that he was able to pray, "Father, forgive them." God was able to forgive because he was not simply forgetting about or overlooking sin. He was dealing with it. He was providing for its just punishment. But he was punishing it in the person of his Son rather than in the person of the sinner.

This is the very heart of God—forgiving but at a tremendous cost.

That does not always sound right to ears that are more accustomed to the thinking of our secular world than to the teachings of the Bible. But it had better be right, since it is our only hope of being able to stand before God when we ourselves die and are required to give an accounting for our lives. We will not be able to plead innocence of sin, because we are not innocent. Our only hope will be the death of Jesus Christ on our behalf.

Can we believe that? We can, since God himself encourages us to do so. The Bible says, "God demonstrates his own love for us in this: While we were still sinners, Christ died for us" (Rom 5:8). This is not only the heart of God. It is the heart of Christianity.

"*I tell you the truth,*

today you will be

with me in paradise."

LUKE 23:43

2

THE LUCKIEST MAN ALIVE

Philip Graham Ryken

he thief on the cross had to be the luckiest man alive. He was nothing more than a low-life criminal, a loser. He had committed a crime. He was convicted for it, and he was crucified for it. So he had no future; he was going nowhere; or worse, he was going to hell. Yet of all the criminals, on all the crosses, on all the hills in the Roman Empire, he was crucified next to Jesus Christ.

Just before he died, just before he plunged into the abyss of eternity, at the last possible instant he received the gift of eternal life. If he had died on any other cross, at any other time, in any other place, he would have been forgotten forever. But he did not die on any other cross, at any other time, in any other place. He died at the Place of the Skull, outside Jerusalem, on a cross right next to the cross Jesus died on. Because he died on *that* cross, he was able to ask for eternal life and hear the beautiful words that Jesus spoke from the cross: "I tell you the truth, today you will be with me in paradise." He not only heard those words—he went to heaven that very day and has been there ever since.

If that sounds pretty lucky, you can be just as "lucky." That penitent thief did not get anything from Jesus that you cannot get from him. You can meet Jesus at the cross the same way he did. You do not even have to be crucified for your troubles. But you do have to do three things this bandit did.

FACING UP TO SIN

First, you have to admit you are a sinner. Salvation is for sinners. By *sinner*, I mean someone who lives life in rebellion against God. That rebellion includes everything you might think of as sin—like lying, stealing, adultery, and hypocrisy—and a few things you might not think of—like impatience, greed, pride, unforgivingness, and prayerlessness.

You might think it would be easy for a convicted criminal, dying on a cross, to admit that he is a sinner living in rebellion against God. Not so. There were two criminals who were crucified with Jesus, one on either side of him, but only one of them repented. The other criminal refused to admit he was a sinner. The Bible says, "One of the criminals who hung there hurled insults at [Jesus]: 'Aren't you the Christ? Save yourself and us!'" (v. 39). There was no way he was going to admit he had done anything wrong. He was the kind of man who always looks for someone who is in worse shape than he is, someone he can kick when he is down. Even when he was dying a death by slow torture, he took advantage of his opportunity to pour abuse on the Savior of the world.

It is not easy for sinners to admit that they are sinners. It can be the hardest confession a sinner ever makes. We usually try to make ourselves feel better by finding someone who is worse than we are so we do not have to deal with our own guilty consciences. The minds of sinners are confused. They cannot see clearly into their own hearts. They do not realize how rebellious they are. They do not understand how much God hates sin.

That is what makes the confession of the penitent criminal, the criminal who became Jesus' friend, so amazing. He said to the unrepentant criminal who was hurling insults at Jesus, "Don't you fear

God, since you are under the same sentence? We are punished justly, for we are getting what our deeds deserve." He admitted he was a sinner. He admitted that it was right for him to die for his sins. He admitted that his crucifixion was only a matter of getting his just deserts.

He also admitted that his sins were an offense against God, and not just an offense against humanity. Dying on a cross put the fear of God into him. It should have, because a sinner who lives in rebellion against God ought to be afraid of God. Your own conscience will tell you that you ought to be afraid of God . . . if you listen to it. This man listened to his conscience, and he was moved to admit that he was a sinner who deserved to die for his sins. He knew that he deserved not only a physical death at the hands of Rome, but also a spiritual death at the hands of God.

You cannot take your sins with you to paradise. If you want to go there, you have to admit that you are a sinner and thus take the first step to having them removed through faith in Christ.

CONFESSING THAT JESUS IS SINLESS

You will also have to confess that Jesus was not a sinner. That is the second thing the penitent criminal did: he confessed that Jesus is the perfect Son of God. "We are punished justly, for we are getting what our deeds deserve. But this man has done nothing wrong." Even though he himself was a sinner, he could tell that Jesus Christ was sinless. It was obvious to him that Jesus had done nothing wrong.

He seems to have figured that out while he was dying on his own cross. Remember the first thing Jesus said on the cross: "Father, forgive them, for they do not know what they are doing." The penitent criminal heard those words, and he must have been moved by the forgiving heart of God that was revealed in Jesus' prayer. He rightly concluded that a man who could pray for his enemies like that must be a perfect man.

In any case, what the penitent criminal said about Jesus was true. Jesus was innocent. He was illegally incarcerated, falsely accused, wrongfully convicted, and unjustly executed. It was the greatest miscarriage of justice the world has ever known. Study the teachings of Jesus, and you will see how good and true all his words were. Examine the biography of Jesus, and you will see how right and perfect all his actions were. The more you get to know Jesus, the clearer it becomes that he was the perfect Son of God. You must confess that Jesus is sinless if you want to get to paradise.

ASKING FOR WHAT JESUS OFFERS

There is one more thing you must do, and that is, ask for the salvation Jesus offers. One of the remarkable things about Luke's history of the two criminals crucified with Jesus is that both of them asked for salvation. Have you ever noticed this? "One of the criminals who hung there hurled insults at [Jesus]: 'Aren't you the Christ? Save yourself and us!'" This man met Jesus Christ face to face at the cross; he asked for salvation, and he did not receive it! That fact should terrify us. It is possible to meet Jesus at the cross and fail to receive salvation!

How is that possible? Both thieves were bad men, and they both asked for salvation. So why didn't they both receive salvation? How can it be that only one thief went to paradise?

For one thing, the unrepentant criminal was not sincere when he asked for salvation. He was insulting Jesus, abusing him with sarcasm. "Aren't you the Christ?" he sneered. He was asking Jesus for salvation with his lips, but he was not trusting Jesus for salvation in his heart. He did not accept Jesus as King.

But there was another problem with his request. He was not asking for the salvation that Jesus actually offers. "Save yourself and us!" he said. That is to say, "Climb down off that cross and get me out of this mess!" He was not asking for eternal life so much as he was trying to save his skin. He was not trying to get salvation for his soul in the life to come; he was only trying to get protection for his body in the here and now.

Jesus could have delivered that criminal from the cross, of course, but he had more important things to do, like paying for the sins of his people, winning a permanent victory over death, and opening up the pathway to eternal life.

The penitent criminal who became Jesus' friend and was invited to paradise must have understood some of these things because he did just the opposite of what the unrepentant criminal did: he asked Jesus for the salvation Jesus actually offers. He said, "Jesus, remember me when you come into your kingdom."

The penitent thief was asking for an *eternal* salvation. He was asking for something from Jesus in the future, asking that Jesus would remember him when he came into his kingdom. He was not asking to be delivered from the temporary and momentary troubles of this life. He was asking for a lasting and permanent salvation.

The penitent thief also seems to have understood that he would have to wait for that salvation until Jesus had finished his business on the cross. Jesus could not have saved anyone if he had climbed down from the cross. That was part of the unrepentant criminal's problem: he wanted Jesus to leave the cross. But Jesus had to stay on the cross to win salvation. He had to die first before he could save anybody. Only after he had finished dying for sins could he offer salvation.

The penitent thief was also asking for a *personal* salvation. Notice how he addresses the man next to him on the cross. He calls him "Jesus." That is not found anywhere else in the Gospels. Usually people addressed Jesus as "Teacher" or "Master." But this man, convicted criminal that he was, addressed Jesus intimately by his first name. He talked to him in a personal way because he was asking him for a personal salvation.

That is the kind of salvation to ask for because it is exactly the kind of salvation Jesus offers. When we hear what Jesus said on the cross to this penitent criminal, we think the important word is "paradise." It is true that Jesus has gone to prepare a place in heaven for every sinner who repents (cf. John 14:1-6), but salvation is not really about paradise. What Jesus offers is better than paradise. He offers intimacy with himself. "Today you will be *with me,*" Jesus said. Being with Jesus is what makes paradise paradise. As that penitent criminal hung on his own cross, he finally found the personal relationship he had been waiting for his whole life—a personal, intimate, love relationship with the living God.

You can have the same thing. You can be as "lucky" as the penitent criminal was, although the Bible teaches that salvation is not a matter of luck. Salvation is a matter of God giving his grace. You can receive that grace. You can meet Jesus at the cross the way the penitent criminal did. But you have to admit that you are sinful and confess that Jesus is sinless. You have to ask Jesus for the eternal, personal salvation that he offers. When you do, Jesus will give you the same answer he gave to the criminal: "I tell you the truth, . . . you will be with me in paradise."

"Dear woman,

here is your son."

"Here is your mother."

JOHN 19:26-27

3

FAMILY TIES

Philip Graham Ryken

n his first two words from the cross, Jesus forgave his enemies and invited his friends to paradise. Now he has to take care of some family business. In order to understand what that business was about, we need to learn some family history.

JESUS STRAINED HIS FAMILY TIES

It all began with what people these days would call a problem pregnancy. Mary and Joseph were engaged to be married, but before they had intercourse, Mary discovered that she was carrying a baby. An angel explained to Mary and her fiancé that the child had been conceived by the Holy Spirit. They believed God, but it was not the easiest thing in the world for everyone else to understand. People in Nazareth could do a little arithmetic. They could tell that Mary was further along than she ought to be. And if you think that was easy to live down, then you have never lived in a small town with small-town gossip.

After Jesus was born, Mary was given a scare. She took Jesus to the temple in Jerusalem to be circumcised, and she was given this prophecy: "A sword will pierce your own soul too" (Luke 2:35). If you think that is the kind of forecast a young mother likes to hear, then you have never had someone cast a long, dark shadow over your maternity.

Then there was that little junket to Egypt. King Herod heard that a king had been born and felt threatened. So he ordered all the infants of Judea to be put to death. Joseph took Mary and Jesus, and they fled to Egypt (Matt. 2:7-18). If you think that was a fun vacation, then you have never made an international journey with an infant crying in the backseat . . . of a donkey.

Or how about the time when Jesus was twelve and the family went up to Jerusalem for Passover? After the feast was over and Mary and Joseph had traveled a full day's journey back toward Nazareth, they suddenly realized that Jesus was not with his cousins after all. He was gone! If you do not think Mary ran all the way back to Jerusalem with her heart in her throat, then you have never lost track of a child in a shopping mall. Three days later—when they finally found Jesus—he was talking theology with the scholars at the temple. His mother said, "Son, why have you treated us like this? Your father and I have been anxiously searching for you." "And after all we've done for you!" she might have added.

Jesus simply said, with some astonishment, "Didn't you know I had to be in my Father's house?" (Luke 2:41-50).

I am not saying that Jesus was a problem child, although there were times when it may have seemed that way to his parents. Jesus was a good boy; the Bible says that he obeyed his parents (Luke 2:51). But make no mistake: as Jesus was growing up, his unique identity as the Son of God and his unique ministry as the Savior of the world did put a strain on his family ties.

All of that was nothing compared to what the family went through when Jesus began his teaching ministry. He abandoned the family business to become an itinerant preacher. If you think that was easy to accept, then you have never had a child quit a steady job in order to freelance. One of the first things Jesus did in his new career was alienate his neighbors, declaring that "no prophet is accepted in his home town" (Luke 4:24). They drove him out of town, of course. That must have been something for the women to talk about when they gathered to draw water from the well in Nazareth.

Then there was the time when Mary tried to help Jesus with his ministry. They were at a wedding in Cana, and the host had run out of wine. Mary suggested that Jesus should do something about it. You can hear the rebuke in Jesus' voice: "Dear woman, why do you involve me? My time has not yet come" (John 2:4). His identity as the Son of God had to take precedence over his identity as the son of Mary.

Or how about the time Mary and the rest of her boys heard that Jesus was teaching in a nearby town? There was a large crowd, and they had to wait around outside for a while. Finally someone sent a message to Jesus: "'Your mother and brothers are standing outside, wanting to speak to you.' He replied, 'Who is my mother, and who are my brothers?' Pointing to his disciples, he said, 'Here are my mother and my brothers. For whoever does the will of my Father in heaven is my brother and sister and mother'" (Matt. 12:46-50). Jesus was redefining his family in spiritual terms as those who do the will of God.

JESUS BROKE HIS FAMILY TIES

Finally, Jesus broke his family ties altogether. They had been strained before, but they were broken at the cross. What anguish Mary endured at the cross where her eldest son was crucified! "Dear woman," Jesus said to Mary. Not even "mother," as a son ought to say, but just "woman." "Here is your son." Mary was no longer to be his mother, and Jesus was no longer to be her son.

Right up until that moment, Mary may well have held out the hope that her son would not have to die. She knew that Jesus had the power to perform miracles. She knew that he could call upon legions of angels to deliver him. She knew that Jesus could even get himself down from the cross. But when he said, "Dear woman, here is your son," she knew that Jesus was taking his leave of her in order to die. His words to her from the cross must have been the soul-piercing sword she had dreaded for so long.

Those words may have been like a sword, but there was also tenderness in them. *"Dear* woman," he called her. Jesus was speaking to Mary with real affection, speaking to her in love. It was really because of his great love for her that he said what he said. Jesus was committing Mary to the care of the disciple whom he loved. That disciple was probably John himself, who was an eyewitness of the crucifixion and a recipient of the love of Christ. John was to become like a son to Mary and was to treat her like his own mother. And John did just what Jesus had told him to do. "From that time on, this disciple took her into his home" (v. 27).

Jesus teaches us by this example to love our mothers. That is so obvious, it seems unnecessary to say it. Yet it needs to be said because we live in a culture that believes that family ties are made to be broken. Robertson McQuilkin gives this glimpse of contemporary attitudes about loving family members:

> I attended a workshop in which an . . . expert told us that there were two reasons people keep a family member at home rather than in a nursing facility: economic necessity or feelings of guilt. Afterwards I spoke with her privately, trying to elicit some other possible motive for keeping someone at home. But she insisted those were the only two motives. Finally I asked, "What about love?" "Oh, she replied, "we put that under guilt." So much for love.[1]

We live in a culture that devalues the old and infirm, even discards them.

Jesus teaches us to do just the opposite. He teaches us to love our siblings, cherish our children, and honor our parents (cf. Exod.

20:12). Jesus teaches us to provide for the needs of our family members, especially as they grow old. Even though Jesus is at the point where he can no longer care for his mother himself, he entrusts her to one of his most trusted friends. He wants his mother to have a place to live and food to eat. He also wants her to have the love and support of a family. William Barclay says, "There is something infinitely moving in the fact that Jesus in the agony of the cross, in the moment when the salvation of the world hung in the balance, thought of the loneliness of his mother in the days when he was taken away."[2]

JESUS BINDS NEW FAMILY TIES

There was one more thing Jesus did for his mother, and it was the most important thing. At the same time he broke his ties with Mary as her son, he established a new spiritual relationship with her as her Savior.

Mary first met Jesus at the manger. She was the first person to meet him. She felt him stirring in her womb, gave birth to him, held him in her arms, and nursed him at her breast. Mary met Jesus as her son at the manger, but she did not meet him as her Savior until she met him at the cross. Mary needed to lose Jesus as a son in order to find him as a Savior. Mary needed to take her place with the other disciples, standing as a sinner at the foot of the cross. She needed Jesus to die for her own sins.

There is a poem by Thomas Warton the Elder that may capture something of Mary's experience in losing her son at the cross:

> *Beneath, lo! Mary weeping stands,*
> *In tears most pitifully fair,*
> *And beats the breast, where Christ had hung,*
> *And tears her long dishevelled hair—*
> *"Where can I lay my mournful head?*
> *My son, my king, my God is dead!"*[3]

That last line explains how Mary's relationship with Jesus has been transformed: "My son, my king, my God." At the beginning Jesus was her son. Now he is her God and King, for she has met him at the cross.

If Mary needed to meet Jesus at the cross, then you need to meet him there too. If Mary needed to stand as a sinner at the cross, then you need to stand as a sinner at the cross. If Mary needed Jesus to die for her sins, then you need Jesus to die for your sins. If Mary needed to trust in Jesus for her salvation, then you need to trust in Jesus for your salvation.

Once you have met Jesus at the cross that way, something wonderful happens. You become a member of God's family. That is how it was for Mary. After Jesus died, was raised from the dead, and was taken into heaven, the first Christians gathered to pray in the upper room of a building on the Mount of Olives. The Bible mentions the names of some of the disciples who were there. Then it says, "They all joined together constantly in prayer, along with the women and Mary the mother of Jesus, and with his brothers" (Acts 1:14). That is a snapshot of Mary in her new family. She is with her brothers and sisters in Christ, praising God for the salvation that they all share together in Jesus Christ. The old family ties have been broken, but Jesus has established new family ties.

You can belong to that same family. If you meet Jesus at the cross the way Mary did, admitting that you are a sinner and trusting that Jesus died on the cross for your sins, then you will be welcomed into God's family. When you accept the salvation that Jesus offers, God adopts you into his family as his own son or daughter.

God's daughters and sons discover that their new family ties are stronger than any they have ever experienced before. If you come from a broken family, then Jesus invites you to participate in the family you have often longed for. He invites you to receive more support, affection, intimacy, and joy than you have ever dared to dream were possible. If you come from a strong and loving family, you will find that the ties in your new spiritual family are even stronger and better than those old family ties. The new family ties are stronger because they are bound by the love of God himself. And they are better because they cannot be broken, even by death.

"I am thirsty."

JOHN 19:28

4

HUMAN AFTER ALL

Philip Graham Ryken

esus Christ now turns his attention to his own suffering. In his first three words from the cross he gave rich legacies to those who were with him when he died. To his executioners, he gave an unconditional pardon. To a condemned criminal, he gave an undeserved paradise. To his mother, he gave the care and protection of the best of his friends.

Now we come to the fourth word of Jesus from the cross: "I thirst." That death-thirst tells us something about who Jesus is and about what he was doing on the cross. Jesus was not finished disposing of his estate. This fourth word gives a clue about one more thing Jesus gave to his people in his death: living water.

A HUMAN THIRST

The thirst of Jesus Christ was a genuine thirst. Wounded men are often thirsty. As their lifeblood drains away, their fluid levels are depleted and they crave liquids. That is especially the case when a man is crucified, for crucifixion is a long, slow dehydration.

If the thirst of Jesus Christ was a genuine thirst, then it was a human thirst. God does not get thirsty. He is never short on fluids. Angels do not get thirsty. They are spiritual beings who do not experience physical lack. Among rational beings, only human beings have the capacity for thirst. The thirst of Jesus Christ on the cross was the thirst of a dying *man*. It was proof that he was human after all.

The Bible teaches that Jesus Christ was and is both fully God and fully man. We needed Jesus to be a man. If he was going to save us, if he was going to die in our place, if he was going to pay for the sins we were supposed to pay for, then he needed to be one of us to do it.

Most secular people do not have much trouble accepting that Jesus was a man. Even most people who do not have a personal relationship with God will at least accept the fact that a man named Jesus of Nazareth actually walked on this earth. After all, Jesus is the best-known figure of the ancient world. There is such a vast quantity of reliable historical evidence about his life that his existence cannot seriously be rejected.

It is different for Christians. Christians *do* have difficulty with the humanity of Jesus Christ. If secular people tend to doubt that Jesus is really God, Christians tend to forget that he really became a man. Try as we may, we cannot quite believe that Jesus was a real human being who walked on this earth. We forget that Jesus was sweaty and dusty, that he grew tired and hungry, that he had bodily functions. There is something scandalous about the truth that God became a man in Jesus Christ, and most scandalous of all that he died on a cross.

For us to hear Christ say that he was thirsty on the cross is to be reminded how completely he entered into our humanity. Jesus *was* thirsty! You and I know what it means to thirst. We have been thirsty before, because we live in bodies that get thirsty. We have been thirsty in the desert perhaps, or thirsty after a long hike, or thirsty after playing basketball, or thirsty during the dog days of August. Jesus thirsted on the cross, just as we thirst. He was human after all.

A PROMISED THIRST

We can almost understand why Jesus had to become a man. In order to save us, he had to become one of us. But why does it matter that

Jesus was thirsty on the cross? It mattered because it showed that Jesus was the Savior God had promised to send. It was "so that the Scripture would be fulfilled" that Jesus said, "I am thirsty."

We know that Jesus really is the Savior of the world because he is just the kind of Savior the prophets said he would be. Jesus Christ fulfilled all the qualifications of the Messiah that God had given in the Old Testament. The more you read the Old Testament and the more you get to know Jesus Christ, the more obvious it becomes that he is the Savior God promised he would send.

The Old Testament promised that the Savior would be betrayed by an intimate friend (Ps. 41:9). Jesus was betrayed by the kiss of one of his disciples (Matt. 26:48-49).

The Old Testament promised that the Savior would be totally innocent (Isa. 53:9). When Pontius Pilate condemned Jesus to die he said, "I find no basis for a charge against him" (John 18:38).

The Old Testament promised that the Savior would be mocked (Ps. 22:7-8). Jesus was blindfolded, spat upon, insulted, slapped around, and crowned with thorns (Mark 15:16-20).

The Old Testament promised that the Savior would be counted as a criminal (Isa. 53:12). Jesus was crucified with two criminals, one on his right and the other on his left (Luke 23:32-33).

The Old Testament promised that the Savior would have his hands and feet pierced (Ps. 22:16). When Jesus was crucified, nails were driven through his hands and his feet (John 19:18).

The Old Testament promised that wicked men would gamble for the Savior's clothes (Ps. 22:18). The soldiers who crucified Jesus "divided up his clothes by casting lots" (Luke 23:34).

The Old Testament promised that the Savior would be God-forsaken (Ps. 22:1), that his bones would not be broken (Ps. 34:20), that he would be buried in a rich man's tomb (Isa. 53:9). All these things came to pass as well. Jesus cried out, "My God, my God, why have you forsaken me?" (Matt. 27:46). A sword pierced Jesus in the side, but his bones were left unbroken (John 19:31-36). Jesus was buried in the garden tomb of a nobleman named Joseph of Arimathea (Matt. 27:57-60). All these things and many others were prophesied centuries before Jesus walked on this earth. They were all fulfilled in his sufferings and death. That is a remarkable affirmation of the unique identity of Jesus Christ.

There was even a prophecy about the thirst of the Savior. King David wrote about it in Psalm 22:14-15: "I am poured out like water. . . . My heart has turned to wax; it has melted away within me. My strength is dried up like a potsherd, and my tongue sticks to the roof of my mouth; you lay me in the dust of death." That, too, was part of the Scripture that had to be fulfilled. I suppose that if Jesus could have quoted it all, he would have. But he was being poured out like water; his strength was drying up like a broken piece of clay pottery; his tongue was sticking to the roof of his mouth. All he could manage was, "I thirst." It was the death-thirst that was promised in the Old Testament. Jesus Christ was being laid down in the dust of death, and he was thirsty there.

There was even a prophecy about the drink given to the thirsty Savior. The drink, like the thirst, confirmed the promise. John tells us what happened when Jesus said he was thirsty: "A jar of wine vinegar was there [that was a bitter, cheap wine, the kind you might hide in a paper bag], so they soaked a sponge in it, put the sponge on a stalk of the hyssop plant, and lifted it to Jesus' lips" (v. 29). In Psalm 69 David spoke about how the Lord's servant was scorned, disgraced, and shamed by his enemies. Then he wrote: they "gave me vinegar for my thirst" (v. 21). Even down to the beverage, the crucifixion answered the promise of the Messiah who was to come. All these things confirm that the Bible is true and that Jesus Christ is the Savior of the world.

That is just the way Jesus intended it to be. Jesus Christ fulfilled the Old Testament Scriptures on purpose. Why did he say he was thirsty? John tells us that it was "so that the Scripture would be fulfilled." If you consider all the promises that were fulfilled in the sufferings and death of Jesus Christ, you realize that Jesus himself had nothing to do with bringing most of them to pass. He did not betray himself. He did not falsely accuse himself. He did not mock himself or pierce his own hands and feet. He did not gamble for his own clothes or protect his own bones or lay himself in a rich man's tomb. All those things were done to Jesus by other human beings to fulfill the plan of God.

But Jesus himself did say, "I am thirsty." He understood himself to be the Savior of the world. So he made a point of announcing that he was thirsty, just the way the Savior of the world was supposed to be thirsty. Jesus was the Savior from sin that God had promised. So he requested the cheap wine that would confirm the prophecy. By declaring his thirst, Jesus was declaring that his sufferings measured up to the sufferings that the Savior of the world had to undergo to save his people.

A THIRST QUENCHED

In the film *The Empire of the Sun* there is a vivid depiction of desperate thirst. In the chaos of World War II China, the young son of a wealthy British expatriate is separated from his family, and there is no one to care for him. The boy returns to his home and lives for a while on whatever food has been left behind. But his supplies run out, and he is desperately thirsty. Even the swimming pool on the family estate has run dry. The boy returns to the kitchen, which is littered with empty cans, and he feverishly licks every last one to the very bottom.

That is a picture of what it is like to live in this world and be thirsty for God. We are thirsty people. We go through this life panting after something, anything, that will slake our thirsty souls. We think material things will quench our thirst. So we shop and buy and hoard things. Then we discover that we are still thirsty. We think sex will quench our thirst. So we leer and lust and indulge our bodies. Then we discover that we are still thirsty. We think success will quench our thirst. So we strive and struggle and step on other people. Then we discover that we are still thirsty. All those things are like saltwater: they look like they will refresh us, but they leave us even thirstier than we were before.

Some will go on being thirsty like that for all eternity. Jesus told a story about a rich man who died and went to hell (Luke 16:19-31). The man was tormented with such a thirst that he begged for someone, anyone, to come and "dip the tip of his finger in water and cool [his] tongue." The rich man was so thirsty that he would sell his soul for a single droplet of water.

Jesus Christ was thirsty with that same thirst on the cross. He endured the thirst of death and the thirst of hell so he could quench their fires for us. The Puritan writer Matthew Henry put it like this: "The torments of hell are represented by a violent thirst, in the complaint of the rich man who begged for a drop of water to cool his tongue. To that everlasting thirst we had all been condemned, if Christ had not suffered on the cross."[1]

Jesus Christ was thirsty for you so you would not have to go on being thirsty for him. What you are really thirsty for in this life is not things or sex or success or even water. What you are really thirsty for is a personal relationship with Christ. Listen to what Jesus says: "If a man [that is, anyone] is thirsty, let him come to me and drink. Whoever believes in me, as the Scripture has said, streams of living water will flow from within him" (John 7:37-39).

That is quite a legacy. If you sense a thirst in your soul for something that nothing else in this world can provide, then Jesus invites you to go to him and to drink what he has to offer. "If *anyone* is thirsty," he says. Everyone who believes in him receives the water rights to an eternal spring of fresh water. Meet the thirsty Christ at the cross, and your soul will never go thirsty again. Horatius Bonar knew the joy of this discovery and wrote:

> *I heard the voice of Jesus say, "Behold, I freely give*
> *The living water; thirsty one, stoop down and drink and live."*
> *I came to Jesus, and I drank of that life-giving stream;*
> *My thirst was quenched, my soul revived, and now I live in him.*

"My God, my God,

why have you

forsaken me?"

MATTHEW 27:46

5

FORSAKEN, YET NOT FORSAKEN

Philip Graham Ryken

ave you ever felt God-forsaken? Jonathan Kozol has written a book about what it is like to live in a godless society and feel God-forsaken. The book is called *Rachel and Her Children*, and it contains a series of interviews with homeless mothers and their children. One woman, who lived for years in the squalor of a New York City homeless shelter, described her religious experience like this:

> I don't pray! Pray for what? I been prayin' all my life and I'm still here. When I came to this [shelter] I still believed in God. I said: "Maybe God can help us to survive." I lost my faith. My hopes. And everything. Ain't nobody—no God, no Jesus—gonna help us in no way. I do believe. God forgive me. I believe he's there. But when he sees us like this, I am wonderin' where is he? I am askin', Where the [profanity deleted] he gone?[1]

THE SON FORSAKEN

Jesus Christ asked the same question on the cross. He did not use profanity to ask it, but he was asking the same question. *Where did you go? Why have you left me to die like this?* "Jesus cried out in a loud voice, 'My God, my God, why have you forsaken me?'"

It was typical for crucified persons to utter loud cries from their crosses. One scholar writes that what made crucifixions especially gruesome were "the screams of rage and pain, the wild curses and the outbreaks of nameless despair of the unhappy victims."[2] Jesus' cry was not that kind of cry. It was not a cry of rage. It was not a wild curse. It was not an outbreak of nameless despair.

Jesus' cry was not that kind of cry because he did not lose hope altogether. This was the only time he spoke to his Father as "God" rather than "Father." Yet even in his agony, Jesus was still praying. He was still speaking to his Father in personal terms: "*My* God, *my* God." And after all, Jesus' loud cry was only a question, though it arose out of his personal experience of alienation and abandonment. It was the cry of a man who felt forsaken by God, a man who was entering the abyss of death and was about to be swallowed up by darkness.

The question Jesus cried out on the cross was first asked by King David a millennium before Jesus lived. It comes from the overture to Psalm 22: "My God, my God, why have you forsaken me? Why are you so far from saving me, so far from the words of my groaning? O my God, I cry out by day, but you do not answer, by night, and am not silent" (Ps. 22:1-2). The Son of God reiterated that question from the cross.

There was no answer. Neither Elijah nor God himself came to deliver Jesus from the cross. The only answers he received were silence and darkness, the silence of being forsaken by God and the darkness of God's judgment descending upon the earth.

No wonder Jesus didn't want to die. When we see and hear God the Son forsaken on the cross, we understand why he shuddered at the prospect of the crucifixion. "Jesus didn't want to die, either." That is what the advertisement said when these sermons were first preached at Tenth Presbyterian Church, Philadelphia. The ad aroused a great deal of interest, not to say controversy. The church received calls about it from other churches, passersby, and the *Philadelphia Inquirer.*

What the ad said is true. Jesus didn't want to die. It is also true that he was obedient to his Father's will and that he was willing to die because of his great love for his people. But the disciples testify that Jesus experienced a dark night of the soul the night before he died. He was in such great anguish that night, and he prayed with such great intensity, that great, bloody drops of sweat fell from his brow (Luke 22:44). God the Son prayed that, if possible, God the Father would deliver him from the crucifixion (v. 42).

When we hear this loud cry from the cross we can understand why Jesus prayed the way he prayed. When we see Jesus forsaken on the cross we can understand why he did not want to die. The crucifixion was every bit as horrific as he had feared. The terror of the physical torture of the cross was compounded by the psychic torment of being alienated from his Father. Surely Jesus knew it would be like that. Surely he knew the crucifixion would rupture the close, unbroken fellowship he had enjoyed with the Father from all eternity. Surely he prayed to be delivered from the cross because he knew that he would be God-forsaken there.

It has become popular for political campaigners to tell voters that they "feel their pain." Such statements are usually about as credible as an Elvis headline on a supermarket tabloid. A man in a navy suit in Washington has no idea what it is like to wear a blue collar in Camden.

But Jesus Christ *has* felt your pain, and worse. You may still wrestle to understand why God allows evil. You may still wrestle to understand why God would allow a man to slaughter kindergartners in a Scottish village or why God would permit some of the tragedies that have occurred in your life. But do not doubt God's capacity to feel compassion for your pain. When Jesus Christ was nailed to a cross, he experienced extreme physical pain, the pain of dying a death of slow torture. And as he hung on that cross, he experienced absolute spiritual pain, the pain of being abandoned by God to the cruelty of the world.

The pain that Jesus endured went beyond the pain that any other human being has ever endured. It may be that others have experienced equal or greater physical pain. But no other human being has ever been sinless like Jesus was. No other human being has ever known the fellowship that Jesus had with his Father in heaven before he came to this earth. So no one else has ever felt the shock that Jesus felt, in his innocence, when he was forsaken by God.

When you meet Jesus at the cross you are meeting someone who can feel your pain. He experienced your pain and something much worse. When you meet Jesus at the cross you meet a man who knows what it means to be utterly forsaken.

THE SIN FORSAKEN

Jesus did not just *feel* forsaken, he *was* forsaken. It was not just that Jesus experienced passing sensations of alienation and rejection on the cross. It was more than that. The question Jesus shouted out from the cross pointed back to an actual experience, to an objective state of affairs, to something that had already happened to him: "Why *have you forsaken* me?" Jesus Christ could tell when his intimacy with God the Father was interrupted. When that happened, he knew that he had been forsaken.

Why did it happen? Why did God the Father forsake God the Son on the cross? We cannot comprehend it. We cannot explain it. The great theologian Martin Luther said, "God forsaken by God, who can understand that?" If even Jesus himself could not fully understand it, then we cannot understand it either.

But we can at least say this: it had something to do with what Jesus was doing on the cross. What Jesus was doing on the cross was bearing sin, carrying sin, wearing sin. Jesus was taking the sins of the world upon his shoulders. It was as if God had taken a giant bucket and scooped up all the sins of his people—all the jealousy and the anger and the lying, all the rebellion and the stealing and the incest, all the hypocrisy and the envy and the swearing—and dumped them all out on Jesus Christ. "The LORD has laid on him the iniquity of us all" (Isa. 53:6). "God made him who had no sin to be sin for us" (2 Cor. 5:21).

Once he had done that, God the Father had to forsake all that sin. When Jesus was wearing our sin on the cross, God the Father could not bear to look at the sin or at his Son. He had to avert his gaze. He had to shield his eyes. He had to turn his back. He had to condemn and reject and curse and damn that sin. When he carried our sin Christ became "a curse for us, for it is written: 'Cursed is everyone who is hung on a tree'" (Gal. 3:13). When Jesus Christ picked up our sins he became a curse for us, and when he became a curse for us he was accursed by God. God was not forsaking his Son as much as he was forsaking the sin the Son was carrying.

If you want to know what God really thinks about sin and what he intends to do about it, look at Jesus rejected on the cross and listen to Jesus forsaken on the cross. That is what sin deserves: the wrath and curse of God. That is what sinners deserve: to be put to death and damned for their sins. That strikes fear into the hearts of those of us who are sinners. At least it ought to. If God was willing to forsake his own Son for the sins of others, should he not also forsake you for your sins?

THE SINNER NOT FORSAKEN

The forsaking of the Son of God on the cross is a fearful thing, but it is good news for sinners who repent. It is good news because it means that when you meet Jesus Christ at the cross you are meeting someone who has experienced the full measure of the tragedy of human existence. Out of his own experience of physical suffering and spiritual rejection Jesus not only sympathizes with your pain, he empathizes with it.

The forsaking of the Son of God on the cross is also good news because it means that God's children will never be forsaken. The Son was forsaken on the cross. Sin was forsaken on the cross. But the sinner who repents will never be forsaken. You do not need to be forsaken. Jesus Christ went through what he went through on the cross so that his own people would never have to go through it. Everything that Jesus endured he endured on behalf of his people. Everything that Jesus experienced he experienced in place of his people. Jesus was thirsty on the cross so that you would not have to go thirsty for God. In the same way Jesus was God-forsaken so that you might not be forsaken.

There is strong hope in the fact that Jesus himself was not completely abandoned by his Father. Yes, he did cry out to God from the cross. Yes, he did experience separation and alienation from God as a result of our sin. Yes, he was even forsaken on the cross. But he was not forsaken forever. Jesus spoke to his Father one more time from the cross. He prayed, "Father, into your hands I commit my spirit" (Luke 23:46). The bond of fellowship between Father and Son was reestablished. The Son spoke, and the Father answered. God the Father received the spirit of Jesus when he died. He did not let Jesus rot in the grave, but he raised him back to life on the third day. Although the Son was forsaken for our sins, he was not forsaken forever.

Neither will you be forsaken. God will forsake sinners, but he will not forsake you if you will come and meet Jesus Christ at the cross. God will not forsake you if you accept Christ's sacrifice for your sins, taking your sins and placing them on Jesus' shoulders.

Jesus promises all who come to him that they will never be God-forsaken. He said what he said on the cross ("My God, my God, why have you forsaken me?") so that no son or daughter of his would ever have to utter those words of desolation again. Listen to what Jesus says now to everyone who follows him. It is a promise that even if you feel homeless in this world, you will always have a home with God:

> *Do not let your hearts be troubled. . . . In my Father's house are many [mansions]. . . . I am going there to prepare a place for you. And if I go and prepare a place for you, I will come back and take you to be with me that you also may be where I am. . . . I will not leave you as orphans; I will come to you.*
>
> *—John 14:1-3, 18*

"It is finished."

JOHN 19:30

6

MISSION ACCOMPLISHED

Philip Graham Ryken

ave you ever left a project unfinished? Our lives are filled with projects that we have never quite managed to finish. We have half-read books on our shelves, half-eaten meals in our refrigerators, and half-finished laundry on the floor in our bedrooms. Most of us still have a pile of junk left from hobbies that we picked up for a while and then abandoned—half-built model airplanes, half-sewn quilts, or half-used exercise equipment gathering dust in the basement. There is probably an unfinished project waiting somewhere for you right now.

Jesus Christ did not leave the great project of his life unfinished. He finished it. He got the job done. He accomplished his mission. As he came to the end of his life, Jesus received a drink of cheap wine and said, "It is finished." Then he died.

That sentence, "It is finished," is actually just one word in the Greek of the New Testament. The great nineteenth-century preacher Charles Haddon Spurgeon observed that it "would need all the other words that ever were spoken, or ever can be spoken, to explain this one word. It is altogether immeasurable. It is high; I cannot attain to it. It is deep; I cannot fathom it."[1]

FINISHED SUFFERING

What did Jesus mean when he said, "It is finished"? One thing he meant was that he was through with his earthly suffering. From beginning to end, Jesus Christ lived a life of suffering. From the moment he left the heavenly palaces of light to the moment darkness descended upon him on the cross he suffered.

Jesus "made himself nothing, taking the very nature of a servant, being made in human likeness" (Phil. 2:7). He was born into a poor family, born in a smelly cave of a stable, for there was no room for him at the inn. His crib was a feeding trough, his pillow straw, his nursery mates some cows and donkeys. But all that is finished now.

Jesus "came to that which was his own, but his own did not receive him" (John 1:11). When he began preaching in his hometown his neighbors threatened to stone him, and they drove him out of town. Even his own brothers did not believe that he was the Son of God. He became homeless, a wanderer, for there was nowhere for him to lay his head. His miracles were not always believed, his teachings were not always obeyed, and his claims were not always accepted. But all that is finished now.

Jesus was "despised and rejected by men" (Isa. 53:3). He was opposed by the priests and politicians of this world. The King of Judea pursued him with a sword, forcing him to become an exile and a refugee in Egypt. The religious leaders sought to trap him in a falsehood so they could kill him. Even his own friends betrayed him. Simon Peter, the best and truest of his disciples, denied Jesus three times and called down curses from heaven to disown him. Judas Iscariot, the close companion who reclined with Jesus at the table, greeted him with a kiss and betrayed him for thirty pieces of silver. But all that is finished now.

Jesus was "a man of sorrows, and familiar with suffering" (Isa. 53:3). He was mocked by soldiers and criminals. They put a crown of thorns on his brow, stripped him, abused him, and crucified him. And then they ridiculed him some more. He was thirsty. He was in agony. He was forsaken by his Father on the cross. But all that is finished now. No one will give Jesus the thorny crown or the rugged cross ever again, for he has finished his sufferings.

FINISHED WORK

That is not all Jesus finished. If the only thing that Jesus finished on the cross was earthly suffering, then his life was nothing more than a tragic waste. And if that is all Jesus finished, then his death was no different from any other death.

Consider the tragic death of Saladin. Saladin was the Egyptian sultan and great military leader of the twelfth century (1137-1193) who defeated the Crusaders of the Third Crusade. When he realized that he was about to die, the sultan called for his standard-bearer and ordered him to lift his burial shroud on a pike and parade it around the camp. The standard-bearer was ordered to say that after all Saladin's conquests, victories, and triumphs, he had nothing left but a white sheet in which to wrap his body for burial.[2] When Saladin finished his life he had nothing to show for it but a winding-sheet.

Jesus Christ did have something to show for his life and death. His death was not just the end of his life, it was the accomplishment of his mission. When Jesus said, "It is finished," he was announcing that he had done his job, that he had completed his task and finished his project. What he had finished was suffering for sin. The suffering of Jesus Christ was not tragic suffering. It was saving suffering.

Before Jesus died on the cross, humanity was in bondage to sin. We were sold as slaves to sin, and we deserved to die in captivity. A price needed to be paid to redeem us, to buy us back from sin and death. But the price of redemption was a perfect sacrifice, a price we could not pay. When Jesus said, "It is finished," he was announcing that he was paying that price in full. Christ died for us, offering himself as a sinless sacrifice, buying back our freedom by paying sin's price.

The word that Jesus spoke ("It is finished") was used by the Greeks for financial transactions. A sales clerk would write it on a sales receipt. What it meant was "paid in full." It meant that the purchase had been made, that no debts were outstanding, that no further payments were required.

"Finished" is just the word to describe what Jesus did on the cross. When Jesus died on the cross he paid the full price for sin. His work of redeeming us from sin was perfect and final. Jesus did all, finished all, suffered all. He made full atonement. Those who trust in Jesus have been purchased back from sin. They have no outstanding debts. They do not need to make any further payments for their salvation.

When Jesus said, "It is finished," he was not uttering a sigh of relief or a moan of resignation. Jesus was announcing and proclaiming victory. He was giving a shout of joy and triumph, a shout of jubilation and exultation, the shout of a victor and a champion. "I did it!" Jesus was saying. The cross was Jesus Christ's job well done. It was his lifetime achievement. It was his mission accomplished.

There were one or two things Jesus still had to do, of course. He had to die, be buried, rise again, and ascend to heaven. And there is one more thing he still has to do: return to judge this world and take his people home to be with him forever. But when Jesus Christ hung on the cross and said, "It is finished" and gave up his spirit, his work was as good as done. He was finished paying the price for sin.

The Bible says that Jesus did not die until he was sure he had accomplished his mission. John writes that Jesus "bowed his head." (That is the kind of detail, by the way, that you only get from an eyewitness.) Then John writes that Jesus "gave up his spirit." That phrase is not used anywhere else in the Bible or in other Greek literature. It is only used here because only Jesus *could* give up his spirit. For every other human being death is inevitable. Humans are mortal. But Jesus is the eternal Son of God, God as well as man. His death had to be voluntary, a willing offering. Jesus' life was not taken from him. He gave it up. "The reason my Father loves me," Jesus said on another occasion, "is that I lay down my life—only to take it up again. No one takes it from me, but I lay it down of my own accord" (John 10:17-18). Jesus could have saved himself, but he did not, choosing to save us instead.

UNFINISHED BUSINESS

Is Jesus finished with you, or do you have some unfinished business to take care of? If it is true that Jesus Christ is finished suffering for sin, then you cannot add anything to what he has already done. If Jesus paid it all, then you do not have any more payments to make. You cannot refinish the finished work of Jesus Christ.

There are some things in life that improve when you add to them—adding a couple of zeroes to your paycheck, just to name one. But some things are destroyed when you try to add to them. You might call this subtraction by addition.

Consider the human face in all its beauty and symmetry. The human face is not improved by the addition of a second nose to the middle of the forehead or by the placement of a third ear in the middle of the cheek. The human face is complete just the way it is. To add to it would be to disfigure it.

Or consider Robert Indiana's sculpture, "Philadelphia LOVE," which stands to the west of the Philadelphia City Hall. "Philadelphia LOVE" is a square steel sculpture built from the letters L-O-V-E to signify that Philadelphia is the City of Brotherly Love. You cannot enhance the beauty of that sculpture or deepen its message by adding more letters to it. If you added a *G*, for example, to spell GLOVE, that would not be an improvement. "Philadelphia LOVE" is complete just the way it is.

Or consider building a tower out of blocks for your favorite toddler. When she comes along to add a block to your architectural masterpiece, she will knock the whole thing over. The tower is complete just the way it is. For her to add to it would be to destroy it.

The finished work of Jesus Christ is like that. To add to it is to disfigure it, mar it, and destroy it altogether. There is nothing you can contribute to the payment that Jesus made on the cross for sin. There is no penance you can undergo, no good work you can perform, no pilgrimage upon which you can embark, no punishment you can endure to clear your guilt before God. When Jesus said, "It is finished," he meant it. He meant that he had completely paid the price to release his people from their bondage to sin. So for you to try to pay for your own sins is to deny that Jesus really did finish paying for sin. For you to try to do something to earn your own salvation is to make Jesus Christ out to be a liar.

If you have never asked God to let the sufferings and death of Jesus Christ count for you, then you have some unfinished business to take care of. If you try to pay for your own sins, you will never be finished making the payments. But if you come and meet Jesus at the cross, you can be finished with the debt that you owe to God once and for all. All you need to do is tell God that you are sorry for your sins and that you believe that Jesus Christ died on the cross so your sins would be completely forgiven. If you do that, then Jesus' mission will be accomplished in your life, and what he said on the cross will be true about the price he paid for your sins: "It is finished."

"Father,

into your hands

I commit my spirit."

LUKE 23:46

7

HOMEWARD BOUND

James Montgomery Boice

From very early in the history of the church, preachers have noted that Jesus' last words show that he was in total control of the situation, as he had been in every moment of his life. For these are not the words of an exhausted man, as if Jesus merely died from dehydration, loss of blood, shock, extreme fatigue, or suffocation. Not at all. They record a deliberate act of dismissing his spirit.

Luke makes this clear by recording that Jesus said these words "with a loud voice," not as a final dying gasp. John says that Jesus "bowed his head and gave up his spirit"—that is, willingly (John 19:30). Matthew combines the two ideas, writing, "When Jesus had cried out again in a loud voice, he gave up his spirit" (27:50).

JESUS WAS ALWAYS IN CONTROL

Jesus was in control all through his life, of course. When he preached his first sermon in the synagogue at Nazareth, reminding the people that God had often been gracious in the salvation of Gentiles as well as Jews, the people were offended and wanted to kill him by throwing him over a great cliff at the edge of town. Jesus simply walked through the crowd and went peacefully on his way (Luke 4:16-30).

When he was asleep in a boat crossing the Sea of Galilee and a storm came up that was so fierce that even the disciples, who were seasoned sailors and fishermen, thought they would be drowned and woke him up asking him to save them from the storm, Jesus spoke to the storm, and the wind and waves became still. The disciples recognized his power over the elements as well as over crowds and exclaimed, "Who is this? Even the wind and the waves obey him" (Mark 4:41).

Most impressive of all is the scene in the Garden of Gethsemane when the soldiers who had been sent by the priests came to arrest him. "Who is it you want?" he asked them. "Jesus of Nazareth," they replied. "I am he," Jesus answered. That response was more than a mere self-identification. "I am" was the very name of God, Jehovah, the name God gave Moses at the burning bush when Moses asked who was sending him to Egypt as the emancipator of his people. God answered, "I am who I am. This is what you are to say to the Israelites: 'I AM has sent me to you'" (Exod. 3:14). Jesus said the same thing, and as soon as he said this, the arresting party "drew back and fell to the ground" (John 18:6). They were powerless to approach him. They remained there until Jesus himself started the whole process going again by repeating his first question, "Who is it you want?"

It is the same at the very end. In the passage we are studying we see Jesus in the last moment of his life simply dismissing his spirit into the hands of God. "Father, into your hands I commit my spirit." He was in total control of every circumstance throughout his entire life.

None of us can die this way. It is possible for us to commit suicide, using some external means to snuff out our life. We can poison ourselves, shoot ourselves with a gun, or do something else that will extinguish our lives. But we cannot simply dismiss our spirits as Jesus did.

NO CONFLICT IN THE GODHEAD

There is another thing we can learn from this last saying of Jesus from the cross, and that is: the death of Jesus did not result from any conflict in the Godhead. We might have thought so because of Jesus' previous statement, "My God, my God, why have you forsaken me?" But here we learn that whatever was in view then, it was not because of any conflict within God. Here Jesus is speaking to his Father with that same confident familiarity he had known throughout his ministry.

There is a mistaken view of what the atonement was about that supposes such a conflict. It goes like this: The Father is supposed to be a God of justice whose fierce wrath causes him to set his heart against sinful people. He is going to punish them in hell forever for their sin. But then Jesus comes along and pleads with God, "Don't do that. Let's save them instead. I'll even go and die in their place." The Holy Spirit casts his vote with Jesus, saying, "I think Jesus is right. That's the best plan." So God agrees.

It was never like that, of course. The plan of salvation was established in the mind of God from before the foundation of the world, and it was carried out in time by the three persons of the Godhead working together in perfect harmony.

First, God the Father determined to send God the Son to be the Savior.

Second, Jesus became the Savior in time by his incarnation and by dying in our place for our sins.

Third, the Holy Spirit applies the benefits of Jesus' death to the individual by creating new life within that man or woman and thus leading the person to place his or her faith in the Savior.

In these last words of Jesus from the cross we find that whatever we may have understood from the Lord's cry of desolation—"My God, my God, why have you forsaken me?"—whatever may have happened, this much at least is true: God had never ceased to be Jesus' Father. It was as Jesus' Father that God sent his Son into the world to die, and it is as Jesus' Father that God was waiting at the end to receive him back joyously into heaven.

LIFE BEYOND THE GRAVE

A third truth we can learn from Jesus' final saying from the cross is that there is a life beyond the grave. We know this because of the way he spoke about his spirit. He did not speak of it as if it were mere breath that he would breathe out for the last time and then die, though "spirit" (*pneuma*) does mean "breath." That is the way animals die, but it is not like that for men and women who are made in God's image and are intended for eternal life with him. Nor did he infer the death of his spirit, as if he were passing into nothingness. He did not teach annihilation. Not at all.

Jesus spoke instead of delivering his spirit into the hands of God the Father, thereby indicating that the spirit, the immortal part of all men and women, survives death. It is of overwhelming importance for us to know what happens to it in the life to come.

Are you prepared for the life to come? Remember that Jesus, who knew what he was talking about because he came from there, not only taught that there is a heaven to which his own will go and in which he is preparing a place for them. He also taught about hell as a place equally prepared for those who reject him and who persist in their sins in defiance of the moral laws of God. He said he had come to give his life as an atonement for sin. He urges us to turn from sin and trust him as the one and only Savior. He asked poignantly, "What good will it be for a man if he gains the whole world, yet forfeits his soul?" (Matt. 16:26).

DYING AS JESUS DID

The fourth lesson from Jesus' words is that as he died, commending his spirit to God, so may we die in like faith. We can echo Jesus' words, knowing that as we pass from this life trusting Jesus' death on our behalf, we pass into the loving hands of the Father who is waiting in heaven to receive us to himself.

This is how the saints of all ages have died, many with these very words on their lips. These were the dying words of Stephen, the first Christian martyr (Acts 7:59); Polycarp, the bishop of Smyrna who was martyred in A.D. 156 at the age of eighty-six; Martin Luther, the great Protestant reformer; Philipp Melanchthon, Luther's steady coworker and friend; Jerome of Prague; John Hus, who was burned at the stake for his faith a century before the Reformation; and an almost endless list of saints.

When Hus was condemned by the Council of Constance in 1415, the bishop who conducted the ceremony ended with the chilling words, "And now we commit thy soul to the devil."

Hus calmly replied, "I commit my spirit into thy hands, Lord Jesus Christ; unto thee I commend my spirit, which thou hast redeemed."

HOW TO DIE WELL

There is one last thing I want to say about this text, and it is how a Christian, in spite of his or her fears about death, can die well. Have you noticed that when Jesus said, "Father, into your hands I commit my spirit," he was quoting Scripture, just as we do when we say the same words? The words come from Psalm 31, which says, "Into your hands I commit my spirit; redeem me, O LORD, the God of truth" (v. 5).

This shows what Jesus was doing on the cross, particularly in these last moments. He was reflecting on Scripture. And not only on Psalm 31! "My God, my God, why have you forsaken me?," the fifth of these sayings, comes from Psalm 22:1. In my opinion, the words "it is finished," the sixth of these sayings, come from the end of the same psalm, since the words "he has done it" (v. 31) can be equally well translated, "it is finished." Even the words "I am thirsty" were spoken, according to John who records them, so that Psalm 69:21 might be fulfilled (see John 19:28). That verse says, "They put gall in my food and gave me vinegar for my thirst."

Four of these seven last words were from the Old Testament. Only

Jesus' direct addresses to God on behalf of the soldiers, to the dying thief, and to his mother and the beloved disciple were not. This means that Jesus was filling his mind and strengthening his spirit not by trying to keep a stiff upper lip or look for a silver lining, as we might say, but by an act of deliberately remembering and consciously clinging to the great prophecies and promises of God. If Jesus did that, don't you think you should do it too? And not only when you come to die.

You need to fill your head with Scripture and think of your life in terms of the promises of Scripture now. If you do not do it now, how will you ever find strength to do it when you come to die? You must live by Scripture, committing your spirit into the hands of God day by day, if you are to yield your spirit into God's loving hands trustingly at the last.

Charles Spurgeon told about an old Christian woman he knew who died in the night but who left by her bedside a poem that she had apparently had strength to write just before she got ready for bed and rested her head upon her pillow for the final time.

> Since Jesus is mine, I'll not fear undressing,
> But gladly put off these garments of clay;
> To die in the Lord is a covenant blessing,
> Since Jesus to glory through death led the way.[1]

That is the Christian's hope. And it is a great hope. But it is ours only because Jesus went through all we have been writing about in this book, dying in our place.

PART TWO

THE REAL

LAST WORDS

OF

CHRIST

"Why are you crying?

Who is it you

are looking for?"

JOHN 20:15

8

A WORD FOR THE SEEKER

Philip Graham Ryken

ood Friday is the time of year when many Christians remember that Jesus of Nazareth was crucified by Roman soldiers outside Jerusalem. It is common for ministers to present messages on Christ's words from the cross—the "seven last words of Christ," as they are sometimes called. But when you think about it, the seven words Jesus spoke from the cross were not his last words at all. He had much more to say to his disciples *after* he rose from the dead. That is what the second part of this book is about. We might think of the next seven chapters as "The *Real* Last Words of Christ."

WHO WAS MARY MAGDALENE?

The first person to whom Jesus spoke after he rose from the dead was Mary Magdalene. It is sometimes said that Mary was a wanton woman. This idea first appears in the Babylonian Talmud, which confuses Mary Magdalene with the Virgin Mary and depicts her as a common prostitute. In the Middle Ages the worship of Mary Magdalene became a religious cult, fueled by works such as *The Golden Legend of the Lives of the Saints* by Jacobus de Voragine.

> The child of noble parents, Mary is said in this account to have received her name for her castle at Magdalo; her brother,

Lazarus, a knight, possesses Jerusalem, and her sister, Martha, owns the town of Bethany. After her debauchery, conversion, and commission to tell of the Resurrection, she is persecuted with the disciples. Fourteen years after the Passion, she is set adrift in a rudderless boat to be drowned with Martha, Lazarus, and St. Maximin, but God brings them safely to Marseilles, where Mary astonishes the populace by her beauty and her elegant preaching and where she eventually causes a miraculous conception and raises the queen from death. She then retires to the desert for thirty years of penance, fed only by the songs of angels.[1]

Obviously, Voragine's account tells more about life in medieval Europe than the life of Mary Magdalene. There is even a medieval play (*Mary Magdalen*) in which Mary sings to her "valentynes" in a tavern before being converted by an angel.

These fanciful errors have continued to the present day. They reappear in the Nikos Kazantzakis novel *The Last Temptation of Christ*. In that book, as well as in the infamous film later produced by Martin Scorsese that is based on it, the Magdalene is a source of sexual temptation for Jesus.

The problem with all these stories is that they have no basis in fact. The Bible does not even say Mary Magdalene was a loose woman. The story of her conversion says simply that "seven demons had come out" of her (Luke 8:2). The true story of Mary Magdalene is simpler, more beautiful, and much more important than any legend.

"WOMAN, WHY ARE YOU CRYING?"

If there is one truth in all the falsehoods about Mary Magdalene, it is that she was in love with Jesus. We know she was in love because of what she did when he died. "Early on the first day of the week, while it was still dark, Mary of Magdala went to the tomb [of Jesus Christ]" (John 20:1). The first thing Mary saw was that the massive stone at the entrance of the tomb had been rolled away. So she ran to fetch some of Jesus' disciples, and they discovered that the tomb was empty (vv. 2-8).

Then Mary was left alone with her grief. The Bible says, "the disciples went back to their homes, but Mary stood outside the tomb crying" (vv. 10-11). As she cried, she peeked into the tomb and saw two angels sitting where Jesus' body had been. They asked her, "Woman, why are you crying?" (v. 13). Mary was crying because she had a broken heart. She had seen Jesus brutally executed and hastily buried. She had lost the love of her life, the dearest friend she'd ever had.

To compound Mary's grief, someone had apparently added insult to injury. She was already distressed because of Jesus' death. But now, as was often the case in the ancient world, Jesus' grave had been desecrated by robbers, or so it seemed. Mary's words to the angels were bitter: "They have taken my Lord away, and I don't know where they have put him" (v. 13).

Not even death brought Mary's love to an end. Everything else had been taken away, but not her love for Jesus. So when she meets the man she mistakes for the gardener she says, "Sir, if you have carried him away, tell me where you have put him, and I will get him" (v. 15). Mary does not even mention Jesus by name. She just says, "him . . . him . . . him"—"carried him . . . put him . . . get him." All Mary's thoughts are consumed with the man she loves.

The intensity of her love for Jesus is captured in these lines from the English poet Richard Crashaw (1612-1649):

> *Show me himself, himself (bright Sir). O show*
> *Which way my poor tears to himself may go.*

Mary wanted to give Jesus a proper burial. One of the other Gospels explains that she was carrying spices with her to complete the embalming process (Luke 24:1). Mary was as devoted to Jesus in his death as she was in his life. She did not love him with a sentimental love, a romantic love, a jealous love, or an erotic love. She loved him with pure spiritual passion. But now Jesus is dead, and Mary weeps.

"WHO IS IT YOU ARE LOOKING FOR?"

Jesus met Mary Magdalene in her suffering. He caught her by surprise. As Mary was talking to the angels she heard a noise, or perhaps she saw the angels look up to see Jesus. In any case, she "turned around and saw Jesus standing there, but she did not realize that it was Jesus" (v. 14). The Bible does not say why Mary did not recognize Jesus. Perhaps she was bowed so low in grief that she did not look up at his face. Perhaps she was blinded by her many tears. Perhaps, too, Jesus was hard to recognize because his appearance had been changed by the resurrection (cf. Luke 24:16).

Mary did not see that it was Jesus, but she could hear his questions. First he repeated the question posed by the angels: "Woman, why are you crying?" Then he added a question of his own: "Who is it you are looking for?" (v. 15).

That is a good question. Who *was* Mary looking for? The simple answer is that she was looking for Jesus. She was looking for "him . . . him . . . him." She had come to the tomb expecting to find his body, hoping to prepare it for burial. Now that he was missing, she wanted to know where he was.

A deeper answer to Jesus' question is that Mary was looking for a dead man. She was not looking for Jesus among the living; she was looking for him among the dead (Luke 24:5). She was not looking for a living Lord; she was looking for a corpse. She was seeking Jesus in the wrong place. The man speaking to her could not possibly be Jesus. Of course not! Jesus was dead. This man must be the gardener or someone like that.

But even if Jesus was dead, Mary wanted to find him. "Sir," she said to the supposed gardener, "if you have carried him away, tell me where you have put him, and I will get him" (v. 15). Donald Grey Barnhouse observes that Mary Magdalene

> . . . was still thinking in terms of a dead body. She had been weeping for three days and three nights and her heart was empty. . . . She had passed through unutterable anguish and had been for many hours without sleep. She had been three times out to the tomb and twice back to the town. [Now] she offered to carry away the full weight of the body of a man, plus the hundred pound weight of myrrh and aloes. . . . Mary was offering, without thinking, to carry away a weight of body and linen cloth and ointments which would go beyond the strength of many a strong man. . . . Here is love, offering to do the impossible as love always does.[2]

Mary was still thinking in terms of a dead body when Jesus confronted her with his living presence. He asked her a question to expose her darkest fears and deepest hopes. Twenty centuries later it still searches the heart of everyone who hears it: "Who is it you are looking for?" Are you looking for a lover? A Savior? A friend? Jesus is all these things and much more. But you will not find him by looking among the dead.

Mary's story is one of the strongest proofs of the resurrection of Jesus Christ. The Bible claims that Jesus died and came back to life. That claim is either a complete falsehood or it is the gospel truth.

We can be sure that the story of Mary Magdalene is not a fabrication. Imagine that you were a first-century Jew who wanted people to believe that a man died and then came back to life. Just about the last thing you would do is let your story depend on the testimony of a woman. Jewish law did not even allow a woman's word to stand in a court of law.[3] Why would John rest his case for the resurrection of Jesus Christ on the testimony of Mary Magdalene, especially when she was grief-stricken at the time? Because that is the way it really happened. What Mary says is the truth. It is the unshakable testimony of a woman who did not believe at first but came to believe for certain.

SEEK AND YOU SHALL BE FOUND

The wonderful thing is that Mary did not remain uncertain for long. She found Jesus almost as soon as she began to look. In fact, she did not even have to find him. He found her.

A mother once lost her little boy at an amusement park. They rode the bumper cars together and then decided to get a snack. By the time she had finished paying for the cotton candy, her son was gone. She looked this way and that, but he was nowhere to be found. He had vanished into the crowds. The woman was frantic. She ran through the park, calling his name with a lump in her throat and tears in her eyes, still clutching the cotton candy. Twenty minutes later she found her little boy sitting on a park bench next to a kindly old man, happily munching on a box of popcorn. "Hi, Mommy," he said. "You were lost!"

Who was lost? And who was found?

Mary Magdalene was looking for Jesus. But she was the one who was lost. Without Jesus she was alone in the world with a broken heart. She was lost in her grief and in her sins. It was Jesus who did the finding. He came calling for her by name. At first he addressed her as "Woman," but when he called her "Mary," she recognized her lover's voice. "She turned toward him and cried out in Aramaic, 'Rabboni!' (which means Teacher)" (v. 16).

Jesus once compared himself to a shepherd and his people to a flock of sheep. He said a good shepherd "calls his own sheep by name and leads them out . . . his sheep follow him because they know his voice" (John 10:3-4). Mary Magdalene must have been one of Jesus' sheep because when he called her by name, she knew his voice.

Do you know Jesus? Can you recognize his voice? Is he the love of your life? Jesus is calling you to follow him. His Spirit is calling you by name. If you hear his voice, you will come to love him as much as Mary Magdalene did. She loved Jesus very much when he was dead. How much do you suppose she loved him—and loves him still—now that he is alive?

"Do not

be afraid."

MATTHEW 28:10

9

A WORD FOR THE FEARFUL

Philip Graham Ryken

ngels are trendy. They have their own books, calendars, notepads, stamps, and home pages. Angels have their own television program, *Touched by an Angel*. They have their own baseball team, now known as the Anaheim Angels. Some angels have even become stars of stage and screen.

During the 1996 holidays two angel movies were hits at the box office. One was called *Michael*, starring John Travolta in the title role. The other was *The Preacher's Wife*. It starred Whitney Houston and Denzel Washington, who played the angel. The angels in these films are no angels, especially in Travolta's case. They are more like human beings. They are irreverent. They wear suits. They have fashionable hairdos. They have doubts and problems. They even seem to have sex drives. These angels might be fun to dance with, but they are not the kind of creatures one is tempted to fall down and worship.

TOUCHED BY AN ANGEL

Real angels are different. They are the kind of creatures you *would* be inclined to worship. I have never seen an angel—as far as I know—but the Bible describes them as beings of dazzling brightness. The response they usually get from human beings is not wonder or laughter but sheer, bone-rattling terror.

Just ask the Roman soldiers who were responsible for guarding the corpse of Jesus of Nazareth. Early on the first day of the week, as some women went to look at Jesus' tomb, "There was a violent earthquake, for an angel of the Lord came down from heaven and, going to the tomb, rolled back the stone and sat on it. His appearance was like lightning, and his clothes were white as snow. The guards were so afraid of him that they shook and became like dead men" (Matt. 28:2-4).

You may not see anything like that at the movies, but that is what angels are really like—powerful, thunderous, dazzling, luminescent. Just a single angel can make a platoon of hardened warriors shake in their boots or faint with fear.

One of the wonderful things about angels is that they seem to know how terrifying they are to mere mortals. Maybe it is the way they can see the whites of our eyes. Maybe it is the way our jaws hang open. Maybe it is the way our knees knock together. In any case, angels are quick to comfort God's friends. "In Scripture, whenever an angel appears to anyone, the angel's first words usually are, 'Fear not!'—which gives us an idea of what angels must have looked like."[1]

"Fear not!" is what the angels said to the shepherds at the first Christmas. As they were keeping watch over their flocks by night, "lo, the angel of the Lord came upon them, and the glory of the Lord shone round about them: and they were sore afraid. And the angel said unto them, Fear not: for, behold, I bring you good tidings of great joy, which shall be to all people" (Luke 2:9-10, KJV). The angel at the empty tomb said the same thing: "Do not be afraid" (Matt. 28:5). Even when God's messengers bring good news, the first thing they need to tell us is "Fear not!"

FEAR ITSELF

The women who went to the tomb on the first Easter morning had plenty of reasons to be afraid. They had witnessed the kangaroo trial and bitter crucifixion of Jesus Christ (Matt. 27:56). They had seen their beloved friend falsely accused, wrongfully convicted, maliciously beaten, and brutally executed. They had watched as his lifeless body was taken from the cross and laid in a tomb (vv. 57-60a). Then they saw and heard the heavy stone roll into the rock to close him up in death (vv. 60b-61). Can you imagine their anguish? Or their fear?

They had more reason to be afraid when they returned to the tomb on the third day. As they approached in the morning darkness, they were startled to see the grave with its black mouth gaping open and the gravestone rolled away. An open grave is always a frightful thing. Who knows what apparitions might come out of it? Then, after everything else, the women came face to face with an angel who sounded like thunder and looked like lightning. They must have been very afraid.

The English philosopher Bertrand Russell (1872-1970), like Sigmund Freud before him, believed that religion is the product of phobia. He wrote:

> Religion is based, I think, primarily and mainly upon fear. It is partly the terror of the unknown and partly, as I have said, the wish to feel that you have a kind of elder brother who will stand by you in all your troubles and disputes. Fear is the basis of the whole thing—fear of the mysterious, fear of defeat, fear of death.[2]

Was Russell right? Is true religion simply the product of our fears?

Bertrand Russell was right about two things at least. First, he was right to say that human beings are fearful. We have good reason to be afraid. We may not be afraid of angels anymore, but we have plenty of other things to fear. There is the fear of failure. The fear of the dark. The fear of heights. The fear of flying. The fear of snakes. The fear of AIDS. The fear of intimacy. The fear of growing up. The fear of the future. The fear of the unknown. And then there is the sum of all fears: the fear of death.

What are you afraid of? You must be afraid of something; nearly everyone is. You may be afraid of losing your job. You may be afraid of suffering. You may be afraid of what is happening to your family. You may be afraid you will end up all alone in the world. You may even tell yourself that you have "nothing to fear but fear itself." That works fine. . . until you get what you were actually afraid of—fear itself.

NOTHING TO FEAR

The other thing Bertrand Russell was right about is that Christianity offers a remedy for fear. Russell himself was scornful of that remedy. He wanted nothing to do with it. In fact, he even wrote a book called *Why I Am Not a Christian*. But the God Christians worship has a word for the fearful. That word is given twice in this passage, both by the angel and by Jesus himself. It is the command repeated more than any other in the pages of the Bible: "Fear not!" or "Do not be afraid."

Whenever you are fearful it is nice to be told not to be afraid, especially by someone you trust. But what is really comforting is to have a good reason not to be afraid. Imagine that you must travel through a dark and dangerous forest on a moonless night. It would be nice for someone to tell you not to be afraid, but that will not comfort you very much when you are wandering in the pitch black and something flutters against your face. It would be much more comforting for someone to say, "Here, take this giant flashlight."

The reason the angel was such a comfort to the women at the empty tomb was that he gave them good reason not to fear. The angel told them, "Do not be afraid, for I know that you are looking for Jesus, who was crucified. He is not here; he has risen, just as he said. Come and see the place where he lay" (vv. 5-6).

The angel began by consoling the women. He understood why

they were fearful. He knew they felt lost without Jesus. He knew they were looking for him and were still grieving over his death. But he also knew there was no reason for them to be afraid. The reason Jesus was not in the tomb was because he had risen from the dead. The angel repeated that message to make sure they did not miss the main point: "He is not here; he has risen, just as he said" (v. 6), and again: "He has risen from the dead" (v. 7). The angel even provided tangible evidence of the Resurrection. He invited them to "Come and see the place where he lay" (v. 6b). Despite the armed guard and the heavy stone, the tomb was empty. Jesus had risen from the dead!

If Jesus has risen from the dead, there is no need to be afraid. The women do not need to fear loneliness because their friend has returned. They do not need to fear loss because what they have lost has been recovered. They do not need to fear grief because the angel has given them good news of great joy.

The resurrection of Jesus Christ calms their every fear. Or at least it ought to. The Bible says, "the women hurried away from the tomb, afraid yet filled with joy" (v. 8). Despite their joy they were still afraid. We do not know why they were still fearful. Perhaps what the angel told them sounded too good to be true. Perhaps they could not quite bring themselves to believe it. Perhaps the very idea of Jesus rising from the dead sounded frightening. In any case, they were afraid, as we human beings often are.

"Suddenly Jesus met them" (v. 9). He met them in their fear. The first thing he said to them was, "Greetings" (v. 9). Literally, what he said was "Rejoice," which is what the women had already begun to do. But because they were still afraid, Jesus repeated the angel's message for the fearful: "Fear not!" or "Do not be afraid" (v. 10).

Unlike the angel, Jesus does not list the reasons for the women not to be afraid. He does not need to; he *is* the reason! Jesus Christ, risen from the dead, stands before them as the answer to all their fears. Because Jesus is alive, the women do not need to be afraid of his body. He is no ghost. Jesus Christ rose from the dead in a real body. It was a miraculous resurrection body, but it was a real body nonetheless. Because Jesus is alive, the women do not need to fear the future. For three days they had been dreading living without Jesus Christ. They did not know what they would do or where they would go. But now they know that whatever the future holds, they will face it with the help and the living presence of Jesus.

Best of all, because Jesus is alive they do not need to fear death. The reason God raised Jesus from the dead was to show that he had conquered death once and for all. It was not enough for Jesus to die for the sins of his people. If he had been crucified, dead, and buried, then death would have had the last word. We could have forgiveness for our sins, but we would have it without the hope of eternal life. Jesus needed to be raised from the dead to win the victory over death. And his resurrection is the proof that everyone who believes in him will also be raised from the dead. Jesus' friends have *nothing* to be afraid of, not even death. When Jesus said, "Do not be afraid!" he meant exactly what he said: "Do *not* be afraid."

Bertrand Russell believed that the Christians were looking for an older brother to stand by them in their troubles. He was right about that too. Life can be a fearful experience. We need a big brother to save us. That elder brother has a name—Jesus Christ (Heb. 2:11-12). If Jesus is the answer to your biggest fears (isolation, death, the future), then he is also the answer to your littlest fears. When you come to Jesus with your fears—each and every last one of them—he says, "Do not be afraid."

"Peace be with you! . . .

Peace be with you!"

JOHN 20:19, 21

10

A WORD FOR THE RESTLESS

Philip Graham Ryken

ometimes we all need some peace.

> "Carol!" I shouted above the din that suddenly surrounded me.
> "Keep the baby away from the windows!". . . I dashed toward
> the house, ducking in and out among the armed men who had
> suddenly appeared. . . . As I ran . . . a second mass of angry
> men were already releasing arrows toward the attackers. I saw
> three of the arrows arcing high overhead and tried to guess
> their trajectory. They all seemed to be falling straight toward
> me, so I leaped behind our house and under the shelter of the
> roof. . . . I climbed the back steps . . . and hurried inside. Carol,
> heeding my warning, had caught Stephen up from his after-
> noon nap and taken him to our storeroom, where an interior
> wall would help to impede any random arrow. . . . While Carol
> stayed beside Stephen, I went to the front door and looked out.[1]

Those are the words of Don Richardson, a missionary to the Sawi
people of Irian Jaya. What Richardson saw when he looked out the
door of his jungle hut was a pitched battle between enemy tribes. He
had come to bring peace but found himself in the middle of a war,
and he feared for his life.

WHEN THERE IS NO PEACE

The first disciples felt much the same emotion after the death of Jesus of Nazareth. They were not at peace. When they met on the evening of the first day of the week, their doors were locked for fear of the Jewish leaders (v. 19), and they had good reason to be afraid. They had seen what had happened to Jesus. They had watched in dismay as he was betrayed in the middle of the night, dragged off to trial, tortured by soldiers, and led to execution. The disciples did not know who would be next, so they locked their doors tight. They were waiting for the footsteps in the hall and the voices at the door.

We may not fear for our lives like the disciples did, but we are not at peace either. Here are two great facts about human existence. First, human beings have a deep longing for peace. Second, we are always at war, the war of every man against every man.

There is no peace in the world. The pleas of the 1960s have gone unheard. Somewhere along the way everybody hopped off the peace train. No one will give peace a chance. There are wars and rumors of wars everywhere, with dozens of armed conflicts around the globe. If there is peace in South Africa, there are troubles in Northern Ireland. If there is calm in Central America, there is chaos in the Balkans. And even if there is peace everywhere else, there is always trouble in the Middle East. Tribe against tribe, army against army, nation against nation. There is no peace in the world.

There is no peace in the nation. The political leaders in Washington are divided on the great issues of the day. Racial tensions boil beneath the surface of American society. There is no peace in the streets of the city. City dwellers are on guard against the threat of violence. Philadelphia, where I live, is known as the City of Brotherly Love, but it is more like brotherly shove. Nor is there any peace at home in the age of the fragmented family. Parent against child, child against parent, sibling against sibling, in-laws against out-laws. There is no peace in the home.

If only you could retreat into the privacy of your own soul! There perhaps you could find a place of repose. There perhaps you could get some peace and quiet. So you leave the world and your family behind to find peace in your heart. But then you discover that your heart is not at peace. The troubles of the world and family have become your own troubles. Worst of all, you have a restless conscience. Deep down you know that all is not well between you and God. You long for peace because God made you to find your rest in him. But you find it impossible to keep the peace because the human race is not at peace with God.

THE PEACEMAKER

Jesus Christ is the peacemaker. He is the God-man who came to this earth to make peace between God and humanity. The prophets called him the "Prince of Peace" (Isa. 9:6). When the angels announced his birth they said, "And on earth peace, good will toward men" (Luke 2:14; KJV). When Jesus walked on this earth he said, "Peace I leave with you, my peace I give to you. . . . Do not let your hearts be troubled" (John 14:27). When his disciples went into hiding, locking themselves up in an inner room, the risen Christ came and stood among them and said, "Peace be with you!" (v. 19).

Jesus gave his disciples a double dose of peace. First, he gave them peace when they were afraid, when they were meeting behind closed doors. Then he gave it to them a second time when they rejoiced at his resurrection: "The disciples were overjoyed when they saw the Lord. Again Jesus said, 'Peace be with you!'" (vv. 20-21). "Peace" is Jesus' word for both the fearful and the joyful. It is a word for everyone who is restless.

Jesus did more than just tell his disciples, "Peace be with you!" The Bible says that "after he had said this, he showed them his hands and side" (v. 20). He was showing his scars. He showed the disciples the places where Roman nails had been driven through his hands into the rough wood of the cross. He showed them the great scar running down his side. One of the soldiers who crucified him had pierced him with a spear to make sure he was dead (John 19:34). Jesus took those wounds to the grave, but when he rose again they were all healed.

The scars on Jesus' body are proof of peace with God. Humanity's war on God is so fierce that something had to be done to turn away the justice of God's wrath. There needed to be a payment for sin. Peace with God could only come through a perfect blood sacrifice. Jesus' scars are the proof that he made that sacrifice and won that peace.

The prophet Isaiah wrote some 700 years before the time of Christ, but he knew then what it would take to make peace with God. Concerning Jesus he wrote, "He was pierced for our transgressions . . . the punishment that brought us peace was upon him, and by his wounds we are healed" (Isa. 53:5). Jesus Christ is our peacemaker. The wounds he received on the cross are the price he paid to make peace between us and God. Anyone who believes that Jesus Christ died on the cross for his or her sins has peace with God. "Through faith, we have peace with God through our Lord Jesus Christ" (Rom. 5:1). "For God was pleased . . . to reconcile to himself all things . . . by making peace through his blood, shed on the cross" (Col. 1:20).

PEACE CHILD

Even the fierce warriors of the Sawi tribes of Irian Jaya eventually made their peace with God. For a long time Don Richardson tried to get them to understand that Jesus had died for their sins, but they had no idea what he was talking about. Part of the problem was that Sawi culture considered treachery a virtue. Once a man had tried to make peace between two tribes. He served as a go-between, paddling back and forth between the two villages and carrying presents. The tribes had just begun to trust one another when the man was invited to a feast. What he didn't know was that *he* was the main course. When he sat down to the feast, he was surrounded by his new "friends," captured, cooked, and eaten. The Sawi expression for this practice was "to fatten with friendship for the slaughter." Perhaps you can understand why, when Richardson read them the story of Jesus, they thought Judas Iscariot was the hero. After all, he betrayed his friend with a kiss.

Richardson did not know how to explain the good news about Jesus Christ to the Sawi until he watched them make peace at the end of a war. The Sawi peace ceremony involved the transfer of a peace child. Each tribe gave up one of its own infant sons to be raised by the other tribe. In this case, the ritual was especially poignant because one of the peace children was an only son. All the members of the tribe gathered around to lay their hands on the peace child and to promise an end to hostilities. As long as the peace child lived, there would be peace between the two tribes. According to the Sawi, there can be no peace without a peace child. And to kill a peace child was not an act of heroic treachery, but the most despicable of all sins.

Jesus Christ is our Peace Child. While we were still at war God gave up his only Son to be raised by our tribe. The shameful thing is that we put the Peace Child to death, which should have made us God's enemies forever. Yet God was so determined to make peace with us that he raised the Peace Child from the dead. It is the risen, eternal Christ who says, "Peace be with you!" The problem with the peace children of the Sawi was that they eventually died and the hostilities resumed. The wonderful thing about God's Peace Child is that he can never die again. Everyone who receives Jesus Christ, God's Peace Child, will be at peace with God forever.

INNER AND OUTER PEACE

Knowing Jesus brings both inward and outward peace. Inward and outward peace both come from the Holy Spirit. Christians confess that the one true God exists in three persons: Father, Son, and Holy Spirit. Sometimes the Holy Spirit is the forgotten member of the Trinity. The reason he seems so mysterious is that he is invisible. He lives in the soul of the Christian. Jesus sends the Holy Spirit to live in the heart of everyone who believes in him.

After Jesus told his disciples to have peace, "he breathed on them and said, 'Receive the Holy Spirit'" (v. 22). Jesus was giving his disciples the Holy Spirit. He had promised to do this even before he was crucified. At that time he described the Holy Spirit as a Comforter, someone who would bring inner peace. "But the Counselor, the Holy Spirit, whom the Father will send in my name, will teach you all things and will remind you of everything I have said to you. Peace I leave with you; my peace I give you" (John 14:26-27). When Jesus sent the Holy Spirit, he was giving peace to his disciples.

There is peace wherever the Holy Spirit dwells. "The fruit of the Spirit is . . . peace" (Gal. 5:22). The Spirit brings inner peace because he reminds us that we have eternal peace with God through Jesus Christ. When we are worried, he reminds us of God's care. When we are fearful, he assures us of God's love. When we are doubtful, he makes our faith strong. When we are lonely, he is our close companion. When we are restless, he helps us find our rest in God. The Holy Spirit brings the wonderful inward peace that comes from being a friend of God through Christ.

The Spirit also brings outward peace, peace between one person and another. True Christianity is always peace-loving. "Blessed are the peacemakers: for they shall be called the children of God" (Matt. 5:9, KJV). The people of God are to live at peace in their homes, in their cities, and in the world. Christians are even supposed to love their enemies. Only the Holy Spirit can bring lasting peace between one person and another. Our natural condition is to compete with one another, even to hate one another. If you want to live a life of inward and outward peace, you must ask Jesus to be your Savior, and he will give you his Holy Spirit.

For many centuries it has been customary for Christians to greet one another with peace. In some churches this is called "passing the peace." Because Christians have peace with God through Jesus Christ they also have peace with one another. One will say, "The peace of the Lord be with you." The other will say, "And also with you." We can pass the peace to one another because God has passed his peace to us. The first one to pass the peace was the risen Christ, who greets all his disciples with these words: "Peace be with you!"

And beginning with Moses

and all the Prophets,

he explained to them

what was said in all the Scriptures

concerning himself.

LUKE 24:27

11

A Word for the Troubled

James Montgomery Boice

word for the troubled? Yes, it was certainly that. But the two people who were making their way back to Emmaus from Jerusalem on the Sunday morning following Jesus' crucifixion were more than troubled. They were devastated. They had been following Jesus for years. They thought he was God's Messiah who was going to drive out the occupying Roman armies, free his people from their bondage to Rome, and restore the glory of the fallen house of David. But suddenly Jesus had been arrested and killed, and their great dream had ended. It had been exciting while it lasted. But their hopes had died with their Master, and they were going home.

What else could they do? If Jesus were living, they might have been able to handle almost anything. But their faith had been shattered, and there was nothing for them to do but go home and get on with the sad task of picking up the pieces of their lives.

The Emmaus Disciples

Who were these disciples? The answer is not as uncertain as many people think. For one thing, the story itself gives one of their names. It is a man's name, Cleopas (Luke 24:18). Moreover, if you use any good concordance of New Testament words and look up *Cleopas*, you will find a second mention of this name in another account of the Resurrection, John 19:25. That verse says, "Near the cross of Jesus stood his mother, his mother's sister, Mary the wife of Clopas, and Mary of Magdala."

It is true that John spells the name a bit differently. He has Clopas, dropping an *e*. But the spelling of names often varied in antiquity, and the two names undoubtedly refer to the same person. So we learn from this verse that Cleopas' wife was also present with him in Jerusalem when Jesus was crucified, and we may assume that she was the one returning to Emmaus with him on the morning of the Resurrection. Her name was Mary. We are told in other places that she was the mother of James the younger and Joses and that she had been a helper of Jesus and his disciples along with other women (see Mark 15:40-41; 16:1; Luke 24:10).

NO ONE BELIEVED

The point of this story, like the similar account of Jesus' appearances to Mary Magdalene and Thomas in John's Gospel, is that Cleopas and Mary were not expecting and certainly did not believe in Jesus' resurrection, even after they had been told about it.

Mary had seen the crucifixion. She must have seen the nails driven into Jesus' hands and feet and heard the dull thud as the cross was raised and dropped into the hole prepared to hold it. She had seen the blood. She had noticed the darkness. She had heard Jesus cry out, "My God, my God, why have you forsaken me?" Finally, she had seen the spear driven into Jesus' side. She would have had no doubt at all that Jesus was dead. Nor would Cleopas have doubted it. He had been in Jerusalem that weekend too, and he may also have seen some of these things.

When Jesus died, Mary went back into Jerusalem to where she and Cleopas were staying. The Passover came, the event that had hastened the trial and led to the breaking of the crucified prisoners' legs. Cleopas and Mary would have observed it like good Jews. It was a sad holiday, but there was nothing to be done about it. They were simply waiting for the Sabbath to be over so they could leave the capital and return to their home in Emmaus some distance to the south.

Something else happened that morning. Mary went to the tomb with the other women to pay her last respects to Jesus' body and to anoint it if that were possible, apparently leaving Cleopas behind to get things ready so they could leave. While she was with the women at the tomb, Mary, like the others, saw the angels and heard them say that Jesus had been raised from the dead. When she got back she told Cleopas about it. But here is the remarkable thing. Instead of believing in Jesus' resurrection, even when she was told about it, Mary simply joined Cleopas in getting ready to go home. She was certainly not expecting, nor did she believe in a resurrection in any form.

And there is more! During the time Cleopas and Mary were getting ready, some of the women told Peter and John what they had seen, and the two men rushed to the tomb, went in, saw the undisturbed grave clothes, and came back to the city with their report. They told Cleopas and Mary what they had observed. But again—this is most remarkable—Cleopas and Mary simply went on packing, and as soon as they were ready they started out for Emmaus. So little did they anticipate a resurrection!

THE BIBLICAL ACCOUNT

Do you think I am making this up? I am not. It is only what the Emmaus disciples reported to Jesus themselves when he appeared to them before they recognized him. Jesus asked them why they were so sad.

"Are you the only one living in Jerusalem who doesn't know the things that have happened there in these days?" they replied.

"What things?" Jesus asked.

They explained that they were talking about Jesus' crucifixion. "He was a prophet, powerful in word and deed before God and all the people. The chief priests and our rulers handed him over to be sentenced to death, and they crucified him; but we had hoped that he was the one who was going to redeem Israel" (vv. 18-21). That was a strange thing to have said, since that is exactly what Jesus was doing. He was redeeming Israel by his death. But they were not thinking of that. They were only thinking of a political redemption. They had expected Jesus to drive out the Romans.

Then Cleopas said, "And what is more, it is the third day since all this took place. In addition, some of our women [this would be Mary, Mary Magdalene, Joanna, Salome, and the others] amazed us. They went to the tomb early this morning but didn't find his body. They came and told us that they had seen a vision of angels, who said he was alive. Then some of our companions [this would have been Peter and John] went to the tomb and found it just as the women had said, but him they did not see" (vv. 21-24).

Imagine that! They had heard from angels and reliable human witnesses. All declared the tomb to be empty, and the angels had announced the Resurrection. Cleopas and his wife understood this clearly enough to have been able to report it accurately to Jesus. But this was so far from their thinking that they did not even investigate the matter for themselves.

WHAT MADE THE DIFFERENCE?

What convinced them, then? We are inclined to say, "Well, it must have been the appearance of Jesus himself. When Jesus appeared to them, of course they believed on him then." But that is not the way Luke tells the story. The fact of the matter is that Jesus *had* appeared to them. He was with them even while they were telling him about the words of the women, the angels, and the disciples, but they were not convinced by his appearance or his presence. They did not recognize him. What convinced them was when Jesus "opened the Scriptures" to them (v. 32).

And notice this: when we are told that Jesus began "with Moses and all the Prophets" and explained to them "in all the Scriptures" what was said about himself, Jesus was working from the entire Old Testament in accord with the common Jewish way of referring to it. The Jews had a word for the Old Testament, the word *tanakh*. It was composed of the three Hebrew consonants *t*, *n*, and *k*, as we would write them, and these stood for the parts of the Old Testament Luke refers to. *T* is the *Torah*, the first five books of the Bible, written by Moses. *N* is for the *neviim*, the prophets. *K* is for the *ketuvim*, or the writings, which is what the word "scriptures" also means. "Writings" and "scriptures" are synonymous. So what we are told in verse 27 is that Jesus used the entire Old Testament to explain that it was necessary for him to suffer and then rise again.

As Jesus did this, their hearts burned within them (v. 32). In other words, they were moved, stirred, convicted, enlightened, and uplifted as Jesus taught the Bible. That is exactly what happens today, of course. And that is exactly why we must turn to the Bible for our instruction and comfort instead of looking for signs and wonders or trying to pump ourselves up emotionally by some other kind of religious experience or entertainment.

Luke's Words for Today

I am sure that when Luke placed this story last in his Gospel, as the Gospel's climax, he was telling us that this is exactly how it must be today. We don't think like this, of course. We think we would like to see miracles. Like the unbelievers of Jesus' day, we want to see some sick people healed, more loaves and fish multiplied, and people raised from the dead. But people had those miracles in Jesus' day, and it did not lead to faith then any more than it does now. This is because miracles do not convince anyone. All they do is cause unbelievers to want more miracles.

Which is why Jesus had determined to be a teacher above all, rather than a miracle-worker. When the disciples wanted him to return to Capernaum to do more healing miracles in Mark 1, since that seemed to be drawing large crowds, Jesus replied, "Let us go somewhere else—to the nearby villages—so I can preach there also. That is why I have come" (v. 38).

That is also why the apostles determined to teach the Bible, though they were able to perform miracles on occasion. When they were in danger of being drawn into controversies over the distribution of food to the widows of the Jerusalem church, they advised the election of deacons to manage it because, they said, "It would not be right for us to neglect the ministry of the Word of God in order to wait on tables. . . . We will give our attention to prayer and the ministry of the word" (Acts 6:2-4).

Paul also made this the pattern for his ministry. When he went to Thessalonica, "As his custom was, Paul went into the synagogue, and on three Sabbath days he reasoned with them from the Scriptures, explaining and proving that the Christ had to suffer and rise from the dead 'This Jesus I am proclaiming to you is the Christ,' he said" (Acts 17:2-3). In other words, Paul did exactly what Jesus did when he expounded the Bible to Cleopas and Mary. "He said to them, 'How foolish you are, and how slow of heart to believe all that the prophets have spoken! Did not the Christ have to suffer these things and then enter his glory?' And beginning with Moses and all the Prophets, he explained to them what was said in all the Scriptures concerning himself" (Luke 24:25-27).

So I offer this biblical advice. If you are troubled about spiritual things, especially if you are uncertain what to think about Jesus Christ—whether he is the Son of God and the Savior and whether you should commit yourself to him or not—the way to have your questions answered and your doubts settled is to listen carefully as the Bible is taught and also to study it yourself. If you do, your experience will be like that of Mary and her husband. Your heart will be stirred, your eyes will be opened, faith will be born in you, and you will become a Christian or grow spiritually.

"Touch me and see;

a ghost does not have

flesh and bones,

as you see I have."

LUKE 24:39

12

A WORD FOR THE SKEPTICAL

Philip Graham Ryken

he Bible teaches that Jesus of Nazareth died and came back to life. It teaches that after Jesus was crucified outside the walls of Jerusalem he was buried in a garden tomb. It goes on to teach that Jesus rose from the dead on the third day after his death. Christians celebrate his resurrection on Easter Sunday.

Furthermore, the Bible teaches that the death and resurrection of Jesus Christ are the most significant events in human history. The reason Jesus rose from the dead was to conquer sin and death once and for all. Everyone who believes in his resurrection will never die spiritually but will have everlasting life. The crucifixion and resurrection of Jesus Christ are matters of life and death, not just for Jesus himself but for every human being who has lived, is living, or will live on Planet Earth. To believe in Jesus is to live; to deny Jesus is to die.

That sounds like important information. It sounds like something so crucial that everyone ought to know it. If what the Bible says is true, then believing in Jesus Christ is the key that unlocks the gates of heaven. The question is: Is what the Bible says about Jesus really true? Did Jesus of Nazareth actually come back to life?

Eyewitness News

One way to tell if something is true or not is to examine the evidence for it. In the case of the death and resurrection of Jesus Christ, most of the evidence comes from the testimony of his disciples.

It is not unusual to believe something on the basis of testimony. In fact, many of the things we know depend on taking someone else's word for them. Do you believe in the assassination of Abraham Lincoln? If you do, you believe it on the basis of the testimony of the men and women who were in the Ford Theater the night it happened. Nearly everything we know about human history is based on word of mouth, even when we find it on the pages of historical documents. History is yesterday's eyewitness news.

Or consider scientific knowledge. Do you believe there is a dark side of the moon? Since you have not seen it with your eyes, you must believe it on the basis of someone else's testimony. What about the cloning of the first adult sheep in Scotland? You have not had the opportunity to confirm that momentous event by your own research. In fact, even if you were to fly to Glasgow today you would not be able to prove that the new sheep is a clone because its mother has since died. If you believe there is a clone, you are taking it by faith. Most scientific knowledge, like most historical knowledge, depends on taking other human beings at their word.

So what about the disciples of Jesus Christ? Can we believe them? The disciples claim that Jesus appeared to them in his resurrection body. Either they were liars, or they were fools, or they were telling the gospel truth.

To Tell the Truth

We can be sure that the disciples were not liars. For one thing, the Bible records the testimony of multiple eyewitnesses of the risen Christ. As in a court of law, the more witnesses the stronger the testimony.

Furthermore, each Gospel tells the story of the Resurrection in a slightly different way. Consider what happens after a fender-bender at a busy intersection. Each eyewitness has seen the accident from a different angle. Although they all describe the same event, they use different words to do it. In fact, if everyone described the accident *exactly* the same way, a police officer might start to get suspicious. In much the same way, the biblical Gospels tell the same story from different angles. The Gospels do not contradict one another, but they are different. One Gospel includes what another omits. Things mentioned by one disciple are left out by another. If the disciples were liars, they would have worked harder to get their stories straight!

Another reason we know the disciples were not liars is that they suffered and died for their belief in the resurrection of Jesus Christ. Most of the disciples met the same fate Jesus himself met—death by torture. Usually people will recant their testimony under the threat of a painful death. Liars, especially, will say anything to save their necks.

A good example of the way death makes liars change their stories comes from the biography of Sabbatai Sevi (1626-1676). Sabbatai Sevi was one of the religious superstars of the seventeenth century. He was a Jewish teacher who claimed to be the Messiah, and hundreds of thousands of Jews believed him. In fact, Sabbatai Sevi was the second most popular messianic figure in the history of Judaism. Religious communities all over Europe and the Middle East worshiped him as the Messiah.

Imagine their dismay when Sevi was captured by the Turks in 1666. Then imagine their shock when Sevi converted to Islam. Under the threat of death Sevi and his closest disciples renounced the God of Israel and became Muslims.[1] They had been lying all along, but the threat of death made them tell the truth.

Jesus and his disciples confirmed the truth of their claims with their lives. Like Sevi, Jesus could have saved his neck by renouncing his claim to be the Messiah. His disciples could have done the same thing. If they had been liars, they most assuredly would have renounced Christianity. But the disciples had such a strong confidence in the truth of the resurrection of Jesus Christ that they took their faith with them to the grave. In the face of persecution and even death they continued to testify that Jesus died for their sins and rose again. Once they had met the risen Christ the disciples could not deny that he was the very Son of God. They were not lying.

DOUBTING THOMASES

Is it possible the disciples made an honest mistake? Maybe they saw a ghost. Maybe they saw the runner-up in a Jesus Christ look-alike contest. Maybe they thought they saw Jesus but got suckered by a con man. Maybe they were well-meaning but mistaken. Maybe they were just fools.

One of the reasons we can trust the testimony of the disciples is that these very thoughts ran through their minds when they saw Jesus in his resurrection body. They were not suckers, they were skeptics. The Bible says that at first they were "startled," "frightened," "troubled," and doubtful (vv. 37-38). They were filled with unbelief and "amazement" (v. 41). Their testimony of the resurrection of Jesus Christ is the strong testimony of skeptics who became believers.

Whatever doubts you may have about the Resurrection, Jesus' disciples had them first. "Maybe it wasn't really Jesus," someone might say. "Well, that is exactly what we thought at first," the disciples would answer. "But then Jesus said, 'Look at my hands and my feet. It is I myself!' He showed us his hands and his feet. We recognized the scars of the very wounds he received when he was nailed to the cross. It was the same Jesus we saw crucified, dead, and buried."

Someone else might object, "Well, it must have been the ghost of Jesus." The disciples would reply, "We thought about that too. But we could see that Jesus was no ghost. A ghost does not have flesh and bones. Jesus did! He had a physical body, a body that we could touch and handle." For the disciples, seeing was believing.

So was touching. Jesus appealed to the bodily senses of his disciples, inviting them to touch and handle his resurrection body to satisfy themselves that he was not a spirit. And eating was believing too. While they were still having trouble believing their eyes, Jesus "asked them, 'Do you have anything here to eat?' They gave him a piece of broiled fish, and he took it and ate it in their presence" (vv. 41-43). Ghosts cannot eat broiled fish. But Jesus can and did because he had a resurrection body.

The reason Jesus went to such trouble to prove his resurrection was because his disciples doubted it from the very beginning. The most famous skeptic among them was Thomas, better known as "Doubting Thomas." Thomas was not with the rest of the disciples the first time they saw the risen Christ, and he refused to believe their testimony until he could see Jesus with his own eyes. Thomas said, "Unless I see the nail marks in his hands and put my finger where the nails were, and put my hand into his side, I will not believe it" (John 20:25). Thomas did come to believe in the resurrection of Jesus Christ. He did not even need to touch Jesus; seeing was enough for him. But it is not fair for Thomas to get all the publicity. All the disciples were Doubting Thomases, down to the last man.

That is one of the reasons their testimony is so trustworthy. The disciples were not simpletons. The Gospels were not written by religious groupies under the spell of a charismatic leader. They were written by men who had both feet firmly planted in the real world: doctors, fishermen, tax collectors. At the beginning they were as skeptical as you would have been, maybe even more so. They had the same doubts and questions you would have had if you had been there. But the living body of Jesus Christ convinced them beyond all doubt that he had risen from the dead. And once their doubts were overcome, the disciples were willing to die for their belief in the resurrection of Jesus Christ.

DO YOU BELIEVE IT?

There is no good reason to doubt the crucifixion and resurrection of Jesus Christ. The great Princeton theologian Charles Hodge (1797-1878) summarized the evidence for the Resurrection like this:

> As the resurrection of Christ is an historical fact, it is to be proved by historical evidence. The apostle therefore appeals to the testimony of competent witnesses. . . . To render such testimony irresistible it is necessary: 1. That the fact to be proved should be of a nature to admit of being certainly known. 2. That adequate opportunity be afforded to the witnesses to ascertain its nature, and to be satisfied of its verity. 3. That the witnesses be of sound mind and discretion. 4. That they be men of integrity. If these conditions be fulfilled, human testimony establishes the truth of a fact beyond reasonable doubt. If, however, in addition to these grounds of confidence, the witnesses give their testimony at the expense of great personal sacrifice, or confirm it with their blood . . . then it is insanity and wickedness to doubt it. All these considerations concur in proof of the resurrection of Christ, and render it the best authenticated event in the history of the world.[2]

It is a wonderful thing to stop doubting the Resurrection and believe. God gives valuable gifts to his saints that skeptics will never receive. The best gift of all will be to see Christ with your own eyes. If you believe that Jesus is risen, then someday you will meet him face to face. How will you recognize Jesus? Probably the same way the disciples did—by his hands and feet. This is how the hymn writer Fanny Crosby (1820-1915) described what it will be like to meet Jesus:

When my lifework is ended and I cross the swelling tide,
When the bright and glorious morning I shall see,
I shall know my Redeemer when I reach the other side,
And his smile will be the first to welcome me.

I shall know him, I shall know him,
And redeemed by his side I shall stand!
I shall know him, I shall know him
By the print of the nails in his hand.

"Do you love me? . . .

Feed my sheep."

JOHN 21:17

13

A WORD FOR THE FALLEN

Philip Graham Ryken

ne of the time-honored fundamentals of the art of boxing is, "The bigger they are, the harder they fall." Whenever a fight ends in a knockout, the loser hits the canvas. Hard. And if you have ever watched one of Sylvester Stallone's *Rocky* movies, you know that heavyweights fall the hardest of all. The *Rocky* movies (except for the first one) all seem to end the same way. In the last seconds of the championship bout Rocky's opponent gets knocked out and bounces on the canvas. The crowd roars, and the ring shakes. The bigger they are, the harder they fall.

THE BIGGER THEY ARE

Simon Peter was big. Very big. He was a major player in the Jesus scene of first-century Palestine. He was the first man Jesus called to be one of his disciples. The Bible says, "As Jesus was walking beside the Sea of Galilee, he saw two brothers, Simon called Peter and his brother Andrew. They were casting a net into the lake, for they were fishermen. 'Come, follow me,' Jesus said, 'and I will make you fishers of men.' At once they left their nets and followed him" (Matt. 4:18-20).

It takes a big man to leave his career and follow God.

Simon Peter was also the first to trust Jesus with his life. One night the disciples were out in a boat on the Sea of Galilee, and Jesus came walking to them on the waves.

> When the disciples saw him walking on the lake, they were terrified. "It's a ghost," they said, and cried out in fear. But Jesus immediately said to them: "Take courage! It is I. Don't be afraid." "Lord, if it's you," Peter replied, "tell me to come to you on the water." "Come," he said. Then Peter got down out of the boat and walked on the water to Jesus.
>
> —Matt. 14:26-29

If it takes a big man to follow Jesus, it takes a giant of a man to step out of a boat and walk on water.

Simon Peter was also the first to realize that Jesus is God's own Son, to understand that Jesus is God as well as man. Once, when Jesus was walking with his disciples near Caesarea Philippi, he asked them, "Who do you say I am?" In a heartbeat Peter answered, "You are the Christ, the Son of the living God" (Matt. 16:15-16).

That was such a good answer that Jesus gave Peter a new nickname right on the spot. Up until then he had been called Simon. But Jesus now said, "I tell you that you are Peter, and on this rock I will build my church, and the gates of Hades will not overcome it" (v. 18). Jesus was making a pun. *Peter* means a rock or a stone. So you might say that Simon Peter was the Rocky of the early church. He was the first to follow, the first to trust, and the first to understand Jesus. He was a very big disciple.

THE HARDER THEY FALL

Perhaps it was because Peter was so big that he fell so hard. On the night Jesus was betrayed, he told his disciples, "This very night you will all fall away on account of me" (Matt. 26:31). But Simon Peter thought he was invincible: "Even if all fall away on account of you, I never will" (v. 33). Big words from a big man.

But they turned out to be false words from a false man. Jesus said to him, "I tell you the truth, this very night, before the rooster crows, you will disown me three times" (v. 34). Peter thought he would never fall, but Jesus knew he was going to fall, and hard.

The historical records show that later that evening Jesus was arrested on the Mount of Olives and taken into Jerusalem for trial. Peter watched the judicial proceedings from a distance.

> *Now Peter was sitting out in the courtyard, and a servant girl came to him. "You also were with Jesus of Galilee," she said. But he denied it before them all. "I don't know what you're talking about," he said. Then he went out to the gateway, where another girl saw him and said to the people there, "This fellow was with Jesus of Nazareth." He denied it again, with an oath: "I don't know the man!" After a little while, those standing there went up to Peter and said, "Surely you are one of them, for your accent gives you away." Then he began to call down curses on himself and he swore to them, "I don't know the man!"*
>
> —Matt. 26:69-74

Peter had left his boat and his nets behind, but he could still remember how to curse like a sailor when his life depended on it.

But a rooster crowed just then, and "Peter remembered the word Jesus had spoken: 'Before the rooster crows, you will disown me three times.' And he went outside and wept bitterly" (v. 75). The bigger they are, the harder they fall.

Have you ever fallen away from the Lord? Have you ever denied Jesus Christ? Have you ever cursed the God who made you? Have you ever tasted the salt in Peter's bitter tears? Big or little, we all fall down.

"DO YOU LOVE ME?"

Jesus Christ has a word for the fallen. It comes at the end of our key passage (John 21). But before Jesus gives a word to the fallen he has a question for them, a question that cuts right to the heart. Jesus asked Simon Peter this question three times.

It happened on the Sea of Galilee, some time after Jesus rose from the dead. The disciples had been out fishing all night, and then they joined Jesus on the beach to have breakfast. "When they had finished eating, Jesus said to Simon Peter, 'Simon son of John, do you truly love me more than these?'" (v. 15).

That question was as painful as open-heart surgery. Notice the way Jesus addressed his disciple. He did not call him Peter. Jesus called him "Simon son of John." After the way Peter had denied Jesus, he hardly deserved to be called Peter any longer. He was too unstable for Jesus to call him Rocky. He had fallen all the way back to being Simon again.

But what did Jesus mean when he asked, "Do you truly love me more than these?" What "these" did Jesus have in mind? Perhaps he meant, "Do you love me more than these other disciples?" since Peter had once claimed that he would follow Jesus even if all the others fell away. Or perhaps Jesus meant, "Do you love me more than these tools of the fishing trade?"—the nets and the boats Peter seems to have picked up again. It is hard to know for certain.

What is certain is that Jesus asks this question because it is a true test of whether someone is a friend of God. The question is not "Are you a good person?" or "Do you give to charity?" or "Do you still kick your dog?" The question is, "Do you love Jesus Christ?" Do you love Jesus from the heart? Do you love him more than everything else? Do you love him more than life itself? Only those who love Jesus Christ are friends of God.

Simon Peter knew that he was a friend of God. He had no doubts about his love for Jesus, or so he thought. He answered, "Yes, Lord, you know that I love you."

Again Jesus asked, "Simon son of John, do you truly love me?"

He answered, "Yes, Lord, you know that I love you."

A third time Jesus asked him, "Simon, son of John, do you love me?" (vv. 15b-17a). Ouch! Jesus really was performing open-heart surgery!

The Bible says that "Peter was hurt because Jesus asked him the third time, 'Do you love me?'" But to say that he was "hurt" is to put it mildly. Peter was grieved. Peter was in anguish. Peter was troubled down to the bottom of his soul. When Jesus asked him the same question a *third* time, it reopened the wounds of his failure. Those three questions reminded Peter of the three questions he had been asked on the night Jesus was betrayed. Worse, the questions reminded him of his three denials, the three times he had rejected the very idea that he had anything to do with Jesus at all. When Jesus asked him the third time, Peter remembered all the bitter tears he shed on the night he denied Jesus. He remembered how hard he had fallen, and how recently.

What was Simon to say? What would you say? Simon Peter knew in his heart of hearts that he *did* love Jesus. Yet he had said that before, only to fall, and he knew how likely he was to fall again. He could only say, "Lord, you know all things; you know that I love you" (v. 17b).

BACK ON YOUR FEET AGAIN

I am not sure I would have believed Simon Peter. If you have ever had someone let you down time and time and time again, you know how hard it can be to keep trusting. But Jesus loved Peter so much that he gently helped him up from where he had fallen. He welcomed Peter back among his disciples. He invited him to follow him all over again. When he was finished with his three questions, Jesus said, "Follow me!" (v. 19), which is a command Peter could only obey after Jesus had helped him back on his feet.

If you have fallen, Jesus is ready and able to help you back up again. But you will not be able to get back up on your own. The reason you have fallen is that you are a sinner. Sin is like a knockout punch. You are out cold, spiritually speaking. You do not love God. You do not serve God. You do not worship God. And if people could see into your heart, you would be ashamed at what they would discover. All those greedy desires. All those murderous intentions. All those proud thoughts. If you want to become a friend of God, you have to admit that you cannot get back on your feet on your own.

The good news is that Jesus came to lift the fallen. In fact, at the very moment in which Peter was denying that he even knew Jesus, Jesus was preparing to die for Peter's sins. That is what Jesus did for all his friends. His death on the cross was more than an execution. Because Jesus is the Son of God, and because he lived a perfect life, he was able to offer his own life as a sacrifice for sins. If you ask God to forgive your sins, he will forgive them for Jesus' sake.

The English poet William Cowper (1731-1800) wrote a wonderful hymn that begins with the question Jesus asked Peter.

> Hark, my soul! it is the Lord;
> 'Tis thy Savior, hear his word;
> Jesus speaks, and speaks to thee;
> "Say, poor sinner, lovest thou me?"

Cowper imagines the answer he would give Jesus. He does love Jesus, but he has to confess that his heart is too cold to love Jesus as much as he deserves to be loved. So Cowper ends his hymn with a prayer that God would help him love Jesus more than all other things.

> Lord, it is my chief complaint,
> That my love is weak and faint;
> Yet I love thee and adore.
> Oh, for grace to love thee more!

"All authority in heaven and on earth has been given to me. Therefore go and make disciples of all nations, baptizing them in the name of the Father and of the Son and of the Holy Spirit, and teaching them to obey everything I have commanded you. And surely I will be with you always, to the very end of the age."

MATTHEW 28:18-20

14

A WORD FOR EVERYONE

James Montgomery Boice

n the great challenge to evangelism spoken just before his return to heaven, which we know as the Great Commission, Jesus commanded his disciples to make disciples of others. They were to lead others to faith through the preaching of the Gospel, bring them into the fellowship of the church through the initiatory rite of baptism, and then, within that fellowship, continue to teach them all that Jesus has commanded them. This commission was for all his disciples—that is, for everyone—and the wonderful thing about it is that Jesus promised to be with us always as we carry this out.

The commission is built around four amazing universals, each marked by the word "all": "all authority," "all nations," "everything [or all that] I have commanded you," and "always [all the days]."

ALL AUTHORITY

The first universal is that "all authority" has been given to Jesus by the Father, specifically, "*all* authority in heaven and on earth" (v. 18).

1. *Authority in heaven.* When Jesus said that he had been given "all authority in heaven," he was making an astonishing claim. The authority of heaven can be nothing less than God's own authority, and the claim is therefore a claim to be God. Whatever Jehovah can do,

Jesus can do, for the authority of the Father and the authority of the Son are one authority. It is this great Lord of glory, God over all, who has promised to "be with [us] always, to the very end of the age."

2. *Authority over spiritual forces.* Jesus' claim to have been given "all authority in heaven" probably extends also to what in other passages are described as principalities and powers, spiritual forces, including those that are demonic. Paul wrote about these in Ephesians 6 in his classic description of the Christian's warfare: "For our struggle is not against flesh and blood, but against the rulers, against the authorities, against the powers of this dark world and against the spiritual forces of evil in the heavenly realms" (v. 12). He was reminding us that the battles we wage are spiritual, and the enemies we face are demonic.

This should not trouble us, however, because these powers as well as all others have been brought under Jesus' rightful rule. Earlier in the letter Paul wrote that God "raised [Christ] from the dead and seated him at his right hand in the heavenly realms, far above all rule and authority, power and dominion, and every title that can be given, not only in the present age but also in the one to come" (Eph. 1:20-21).

3. *Authority over his disciples.* When Jesus says that "all authority . . . on earth" has been given to him, this includes those who are on the earth, including Christ's disciples. His authority obviously extends to them as well. It extends to their conduct, for he has called them to follow him in obedience to his commands. He said: "You are my friends if you do what I command" (John 15:14). If we are not obeying Jesus, we are not his friends; indeed, we are not even saved. Christ's authority also extends to the work his disciples are being called to do. The Great Commission stresses this chiefly. It is because we are under the authority of Jesus that we are to take his Gospel to the world, making "disciples of all nations, baptizing them in the name of the Father and of the Son and of the Holy Spirit, and teach-

ing them to obey everything" he has commanded us (vv. 19-20).

The disciples of Jesus are not at liberty to set their own agenda. They are under "marching orders," as the Duke of Wellington once said, describing his own sense of being under the authority of Christ.

4. *Authority over the nations.* The fourth area to which the authority of the Lord Jesus Christ extends is those nations or people who do not yet acknowledge his authority but to whom he sends us. It is this that makes Christianity a world religion. There were many religions in the world in which a god was perceived as the deity of a special people but whose authority was limited to that people only. Not so with Jesus. He was born a Jew, but his religion is not Jewish. Nor is it Greek or Roman or western European or American. It is an earth-embracing religion, because Jesus has been given authority over all the earth.

John Stott summarizes it like this:

> The fundamental basis of all Christian missionary enterprise is the universal authority of Jesus Christ, "in heaven and on earth." If the authority of Jesus were circumscribed on earth, if he were but one of many religious teachers, one of many Jewish prophets, one of many divine incarnations, we would have no mandate to present him to the nations as the Lord and Savior of the world. If the authority of Jesus were limited in heaven, if he had not decisively overthrown the principalities and powers, we might still proclaim him to the nations, but we would never be able to "turn them from darkness to the light, and from the power of Satan unto God" (Acts 26:18). Only because all authority on earth belongs to Christ dare we go to all nations. And only because all authority in heaven as well is his have we any hope of success.[1]

"ALL NATIONS"

The second of these four great universals is "all nations." It refers to the worldwide authority of Jesus and so also to the worldwide character of Christianity, as I have indicated.

It is surprising that Matthew, of all the Gospels, should end on this note. For Matthew is the most ethnic or Jewish Gospel. It was written to show Jesus as the son of David and the fulfiller of the Old Testament prophecies concerning the Messiah. No other Gospel is so limited to the ethnic climate into which Jesus was born and in which he ministered. Yet surprisingly it is this Gospel that ends on the most universal note. In the Great Commission we learn that the few Jewish disciples who had followed Jesus through the days of his ministry and who were now being commissioned formally to his service were not to limit their witness to Judaism but were to go to all the people and nations of the world with this Gospel.

Whenever the church has done this, it has been blessed and prospered. When it has not done this, it has stagnated and atrophied. Why is this? It is because discipleship demands the Great Commission; it is an aspect of our obedience as Christ's followers, and Jesus blesses obedience. If we are following Jesus, we will go to all for whom he died.

"EVERYTHING I HAVE COMMANDED"

One of the most important universals in these verses, particularly for our superficial age, is the command to teach those we have discipled. We are to teach them "everything" Christ commanded. Today we see what seems to be the opposite. Instead of striving to teach *all* Christ commanded, many seem to be trying to eliminate as much of his teaching as possible, concentrating on an easily comprehended, unobjectionable "core" of teaching. It is grace without judgment, love without justice, salvation without obedience, and triumph without suffering. The motivation of some of these reductionists may be good—to win as many persons to Christ as possible. But the method is the world's, and the results (as a natural consequence) are the world's results. Disciples are not made by defective teaching. The world is not subjected to Christ's rule by demi-gospels.

What teachings does today's church need to recover? Any brief listing of doctrines is inadequate. We must teach the entire Bible. Nevertheless, faithfulness to Christ must involve at least the following:

1. *A high view of Scripture.* In past days liberal teachers undermined the church's traditionally high view of the Bible by saying that it is only a human book, that it contains errors, and that it is therefore at best only relatively trustworthy or authoritative. This weakened the church. But in our day evangelicals undermine the authority of the Bible too because they do not consider it to be adequate for the tasks we face and therefore neglect it in countless areas. If we are to be faithful to Christ's teachings, we must absorb his high view of the Bible as a fundamental part of our theology.

2. *The sovereignty of God.* The English Bible translator J.B. Phillips wrote a book called *Your God Is Too Small,* which is exactly the case with many apparent believers. They are ignorant of Scripture and therefore inevitably scale God down to their own limited and fallible perspectives. We need to capture a new, elevated sense of who God is, particularly in regard to his sovereignty. Sovereignty refers to rightful rule. So to say that God is sovereign, as the Bible does, is to say that he rules in his universe. Nothing is an accident; nothing catches God off guard.

3. *The depravity of man.* People are willing to acknowledge sin in the sense that we are all "less perfect than God" and need help to live a good life. That is not offensive to anyone. But it is not the full biblical teaching. The Bible teaches that we are dead in our sin (Eph. 2:1-3), and so affected by it that even our thoughts are corrupted (Gen. 6:5). And so great is our depravity that we cannot even come to Christ unless God first renews our souls and draws us to him (John 6:44).

4. *The grace of God.* While it is true that in ourselves we cannot come to Christ, and so we are under God's judgment, Jesus teaches

that God has nevertheless acted in grace toward some who were perishing. Thus salvation is by grace alone. Jesus said, "All that the Father gives me will come to me" (John 6:37). He said to his Father, "I am not praying for the world, but for those you have given me" (John 17:9).

5. *The need for good works.* Although God does the work of saving individuals, drawing them to Christ, he does not abandon them at that point, but rather directs and empowers them to do meaningful work for him. Most of Christ's teachings about discipleship fall into this area. Like Jesus himself, we are to stand for justice and do everything in our power to comfort the sick, rescue the outcast, defend the oppressed, and save the innocent. We are also to oppose those who perpetrate or condone injustice.

6. *The security of the believer in Christ.* Jesus was strong in cautioning against presumption. He let no one presume himself or herself to be a Christian while disregarding or disobeying his teachings. Nevertheless, although Jesus cautioned against presumption, he also spoke the greatest words of assurance and confidence for those who did follow him. He said they would never be lost. Indeed, how could they be if God himself is responsible for their salvation (John 10:28)?

"ALWAYS" AND FOREVER

The final universal of Matthew 28:18-20 is "always," or as the Greek literally says, "all the days, even to the consummation of the age." This is a great promise. In the first chapter of Matthew Jesus was introduced as "'Immanuel'—which means, 'God with us'" (Matt. 1:23). Here in the very last verse of Matthew that promise is repeated and confirmed. It is a promise that when we do as Christ commands, when each of us actually does go into the world with the Gospel to win men and women to Christ and to a lifetime of fellowship and service within the church, then

Jesus will be with us through thick and thin until we finally stand before him in glory.

It is not easy to follow Jesus Christ. He never suggested it would be. But it is far better than not following him, for not only do we have the promise of a sure and certain hope beyond the grave and rewards in heaven, we have the promise of the Lord's presence with us even now.

PART THREE

THE

MESSAGE

OF THE

CROSS

"This man

was handed over to you

by God's set purpose

and foreknowledge."

ACTS 2:23

15

THE NECESSITY OF THE CROSS

Philip Graham Ryken

 hristianity is all about the cross. By *cross* is meant the wooden post upon which Jesus of Nazareth was crucified. This was a standard means of execution in Roman times. Two wooden beams were nailed together in the shape of a cross or a T. The wrists and ankles of the victim were nailed to the wood, which was then slotted into the ground. There the man hung until he died.

The cross has always been the central symbol of Christianity. When archaeologists dig through the ruins of antiquity, they have one certain way to identify a place of Christian worship. They look for a cross. When they find it painted on a wall, carved into stone, or even worked into a floor plan, they know they have found a church.

Since the beginning, Christians have identified themselves with the cross on which Jesus died. It is the chief symbol and defining reality of Christian faith.

NO LONGER NECESSARY?

Unfortunately, the cross is not as important as it used to be. At least, that is what many leading thinkers are saying about the contemporary church. George Lindbeck, who teaches theology at Yale, says the cross has become a dead symbol. "A void has opened in the heart of Western Christianity. Where the cross once stood is now a vacuum."[1]

Not that the cross has disappeared altogether. Not yet anyway. It still stands atop the church steeple. It appears on church letterheads. It is stamped into Bible covers and breath mints at the local Christian bookstore. It even dangles from postmodern ears. However, the cross of Christ is no longer a living reality for the people of God.

At a conference in the early 1990s, one speaker objected to Christianity's seeming obsession with the cross. "I don't think we need folks hanging on crosses and blood dripping and weird stuff," this speaker said. In other words, who needs the cross?

It is true that there is something unsightly, even grotesque, about crucifixion. The Bible does not overlook this horror. Concerning Jesus, the prophet Isaiah said, "Like one from whom men hide their faces he was despised" (Isa. 53:3). The cross is as unsightly as it is unpopular. But it is still necessary. Wherever the cross disappears, true religion disappears, for there is no Christianity without the cross.

NECESSARY TO FULFILL GOD'S PLAN

Why is the cross of Christ so essential to Christianity? It is necessary for several reasons. First, the cross was necessary to fulfill God's eternal plan.

There was a time when Jesus himself wondered if the cross was necessary. It was the night he went to pray in the Garden of Gethsemane. He knew his enemies were closing in on him. In fact, later the same night he would be betrayed, arrested, and sentenced to death.

Jesus knew the end was near. Like any human being, he was horrified by the prospect of death. Although Jesus is God, he is also a human being. As a human being, he wondered if it was necessary for him to die such a painful death. Thinking what it would it be like to be crucified, he said, "'My soul is overwhelmed with sorrow to the point of death.' Going a little farther, he fell with his face to the ground and prayed, 'My Father, if it is possible, may this cup be taken from me'" (Matt. 26:38-39). Jesus was asking his Father if there was any way he could save his people without being crucified.

Yet because it was an essential part of his plan, God the Father did not spare God the Son from the cross. Jesus explained this after he was crucified and had come back to life. He spoke with two of his disciples. They were puzzled by what had happened to him. They did not understand why Jesus died on a cross. He answered, "Did not the Christ have to suffer these things?" (Luke 24:26). According to God's eternal plan, the cross of Christ was inevitable.

Christians, therefore, have always believed and taught the necessity of the cross. Not long after Jesus returned to heaven, his friend Peter preached to the people of Jerusalem. He said: "This man [Jesus] was handed over to you by God's set purpose and foreknowledge; and you, with the help of wicked men, put him to death by nailing him to the cross" (Acts 2:23). God knew about the crucifixion of his Son even before it happened. He not only knew about it, he permitted it. He not only permitted it, he purposed it. The cross was essential to his plan for humanity.

This is worth remembering whenever it seems like God doesn't know what he is doing. The trials and tragedies of life are often puzzling. Does God know what is happening in my life? Does he care? Can he do anything about it? The answer is that God does know and does care. And if you trust him, he will do something about it.

The cross of Christ proves that God's plans are good. The crucifixion of Jesus Christ was the most evil deed ever committed on this planet. God's own perfect Son was put to death by wicked men. What could be more evil than that? At the same time, however, the crucifixion of Jesus was the best thing that ever happened on this planet. As we shall see, the cross has brought salvation to the world. If God brought the greatest good out of the greatest evil, he can bring good out of what seems to be evil in your own life. It is all part of God's good plan.

NECESSARY TO PAY FOR SIN

What made crucifixion part of God's plan in the first place? Why was the cross necessary? What was it necessary for?

The cross was part of God's plan because it was the only way to save human beings from their sins. In the words of John Owen (1616-1683), the great Oxford Puritan, "There is no death of sin without the death of Christ."[2] Understanding sin, therefore, is part of understanding the cross.

What is sin? The answer is twofold. Sin is: (1) doing anything God forbids, or (2) failing to do anything God requires.

First, sin means doing what God forbids. Whenever you curse God, tell a small untruth, steal office supplies, or strike out at someone in anger, you commit a sin. You have broken God's commandment against cursing, lying, stealing, or murder.

Second, sin also includes not doing what God requires. God wants people to worship him, to put others before themselves, to care for the sick and give to the poor. With those things in mind, it is worth asking, "What have you done for God lately?" If the answer is "Not very much," then you are sinning by not doing what God requires.

The reason sin is a problem is because God is holy. God is so perfectly holy that it is impossible for any sinful human being to stand before him. Sin brings us under divine judgment. We deserve to be cursed and damned for our sins.

That is why Christ's death on the cross was such a necessary part of God's plan. God wanted to save his people from their sins. But how could he deal with our sin without sacrificing either his love or his holiness? That was the problem.

God could not simply overlook our sins. That might have been loving, but it would not have been holy. Justice would not have been served. Our sins would not have been paid for. Nor did God simply condemn us to die for our own sins. That would have been holy, but it would not have been a full demonstration of God's love.

The place God's love and God's holiness embrace is at the cross. Here is the love of God. God the Father sent his Son, his only Son, to suffer and to die for our sins. His life for your life, his pain for your gain. Here also, in the cross, is the holiness of God. The death penalty is executed against sin. The sins of God's people are paid in full.

The cross of Christ is necessary to preserve both God's love and God's holiness in the salvation of God's people. The German theologian Emil Brunner (1889-1966) explained that the cross of Christ "is the event in which God makes known his holiness and his love simultaneously, in one event, in an absolute manner. . . . The cross is the only place where the loving, forgiving merciful God is revealed in such a way that we perceive that his holiness and his love are equally infinite."[3]

NECESSARY TO SAVE YOU

There is one other way in which the cross is necessary. It is essential for your salvation. Anyone who wants to go to heaven must first go to the cross. Eternal life is God's free gift for anyone who believes that Jesus died for his or her sin on the cross.

One thing that means is believing the crucifixion really happened. The historical records show that Jesus of Nazareth was crucified by Roman soldiers on a hill just outside Jerusalem in 30 A.D. Believing in Jesus' death on the cross means believing that if you had been there that day, you could have touched his cross and received a splinter in your finger. The Christ on the cross was a living, bleeding, dying person. To become a believer is to accept that Jesus Christ lived a real life and died a real death.

But believing Jesus died on the cross also means something more. It means believing that he did what he did for your salvation. It means acknowledging that you, personally, are a sinner. It means confessing that you need Jesus Christ to save you from the wrath and curse of God. It means believing that Jesus died on that splintery old cross for your own personal sins.

Once a woman decided to become a member of the church she was attending. So she went to be interviewed by the church elders. They asked her what she thought it meant to be a Christian. Among other things, she explained how Jesus died on the cross to pay for sin.

The woman's theology was sound, but the elders felt uneasy. They were not sure she was a genuine Christian. This was because she spoke in a casual way, as if the cross had little or no relevance to her own life. There are plenty of people like her in the church. They are Christians in a general sort of way, but they have not made a personal life-and-death commitment to Jesus Christ.

So the elders asked her a follow-up question: "Do you believe that Jesus died on the cross, not just for the sins of others, but for *your* sins?" There was a long pause, and finally the woman said, "I've never thought about it that way before."

The elders explained to her that she needed to confess that she herself was one of the sinners for whom Christ died. That night she believed that Jesus died on the cross for her sins and received him as her personal Savior.

That woman came to understand what everyone must understand to be saved: the necessity of the cross. The cross is necessary, not just in a general way as part of God's eternal plan, but necessary for your very own salvation from sin and death.

. . . who for the joy

set before him

endured the cross,

scorning its shame.

HEBREWS 12:2

16

THE OFFENSE OF THE CROSS

Philip Graham Ryken

he cross has become so familiar that it has lost its power to offend. It is no longer offensive to Christians because they are used to seeing it, talking about it, hearing about it, and singing about it all the time. Nor is the cross offensive to non-Christians. For them it is a symbol of religious commitment, or perhaps a fashion accessory. The cross of Christ has been tamed.

The taming of the cross is a sign that its true meaning has been lost. For as soon as people understand what crucifixion means, the cross becomes utterly offensive to them. The early Christian theologian Origen (c. 185-c. 254) rightly called it the "utterly vile death of the cross."[1]

AN ABOMINATION TO THE ROMANS

The cross was an abomination to the Romans. For them it was a brutal means of execution. It was the electric chair or the lethal injection of the ancient world, and death row is no place for sentimentality. There is nothing pretty about an execution.

Not only was crucifixion a means of execution, it was the most gruesome means imaginable. Marcus Tullius Cicero (106-43 B.C.) described it as "a most cruel and disgusting punishment."[2] It was associated with torture, bleeding, nakedness, and agony. It was designed to kill only after the victim had endured the maximum possible suffering.

Not surprisingly, crucifixion was meant for criminals, and only for hardened criminals at that. The great New Testament scholar F. F. Bruce wrote, "To die by crucifixion was to plumb the lowest depths of disgrace; it was a punishment reserved for those who were deemed most unfit to live, a punishment for those who were subhuman."[3] The cross was for murderers and rebels, provided they were also slaves or foreigners.

All these reasons explain why the cross was an offense to the Romans, so much so that they refused to allow their own citizens to be crucified, no matter what they had done. Cicero claimed, "It is a crime to put a Roman citizen in chains, it is an enormity to flog one, sheer murder to slay one; what, then, shall I say of crucifixion? It is impossible to find the word for such an abomination."[4]

Indeed, there was no word for it. No polite word, at any rate, for the word for *cross* was taboo in Roman society. To quote again from Cicero, "Let the very mention of the cross be far removed not only from a Roman citizen's body, but from his mind, his eyes, his ears."[5] *Crux* was a Latin swear word.

Since the Romans considered crucifixion an abomination, it is not surprising that many of them held Christianity in derision. A fascinating example comes from the Palatine Hill in Rome. There, on the wall of a house, the oldest surviving picture of the crucifixion was found, in the form of graffiti. The crude drawing depicts a man with a head of a donkey stretched on a cross. Another man stands at the foot of the cross with one arm raised in worship. A taunt is scribbled underneath: "Alexamenos worships God."[6] Thus the Romans poured their scorn on those who worshiped a crucified man.

A CURSE TO THE JEWS

As offensive as crucifixion was to the Romans, it was even more offensive to the Jews. According to Hebrew law, any man who was crucified was under a divine curse. This is what the Torah says: "If a man guilty of a capital offense is put to death and his body is hung on a tree, you must not leave his body on the tree overnight. Be sure to bury him that same day, because anyone who is hung on a tree is under God's curse" (Deut. 21:22-23).

The curse of the cross explains why Jesus was crucified outside Jerusalem. Crucifixion was such an abomination that the Jews never would have allowed it to take place within the sacred precincts of their holy city. The cursed death of the cursed man had to take place outside the city wall.

The biblical curse also explains something curious about the way the first Christians described the cross. They often referred to it as a "tree." For example, when the apostle Peter preached to the leaders of Jerusalem, he said, "The God of our fathers raised Jesus from the dead—whom you had killed by hanging him on a tree" (Acts 5:30). He said the same thing when he traveled to Caesarea and spoke to a Roman soldier named Cornelius: "We are witnesses of everything [Jesus] did in the country of the Jews and in Jerusalem. They killed him by hanging him on a tree" (Acts 10:39).

The apostle Paul described the crucifixion in the same way. He went to the synagogue in Pisidian Antioch and testified, "The people of Jerusalem and their rulers did not recognize Jesus, yet in condemning him they fulfilled the words of the prophets that are read every Sabbath. Though they found no proper ground for a death sentence, they asked Pilate to have him executed. When they had carried out all that was written about him, they took him down from the tree and laid him in a tomb" (13:27-29).

What is curious about these statements is that they speak of a "tree" rather than a "cross." Both terms are appropriate, but calling the cross a "tree" serves as a reminder of the Old Testament curse.

Because of that curse one might even say that the cross was an offense to God the Father, for he was the one who had cursed the cross in the first place. It was his Word that stated that anyone hung upon a tree was accursed. God's Son Jesus Christ experienced that curse when he was crucified. Shortly before his death the sky turned black, and "Jesus cried out in a loud voice, 'Eloi, Eloi, lama sabachthani?'—which means, 'My God, my God, why have you forsaken me?'" (Matt. 27:46). Jesus died a God-forsaken death on a God-forsaken cross.

Why did the first Christians call attention to the fact that Jesus died on a tree? The very idea is offensive to the Jewish ear. In fact, in an ancient conversation between Justin the Christian and Trypho the Jew, Trypho refused to believe that God's Messiah could possibly have died upon a tree: "But whether Christ should be so shamefully crucified, this we are in doubt about. For whosoever is crucified is said in the law to be accursed, so that I am exceedingly incredulous on this point."[7]

Yet the first Christians were not ashamed to let everyone know that Jesus died on a cursed cross. They understood that by being crucified, he had taken God's curse against their sin upon himself. The apostle Peter put it like this: "He himself bore our sins in his body on the tree" (1 Pet. 2:24). The reason Jesus died an accursed death on the cross was to undergo the curse we deserve for our sin.

The offense of the cross went all the way back to the Old Testament curse of the tree. The apostle Paul made this connection explicit when he wrote: "Christ redeemed us from the curse of the law by becoming a curse for us, for it is written: 'Cursed is everyone who is hung on a tree'" (Gal. 3:13).

AN AFFRONT TO EVERY MORAL INDIVIDUAL

The cross was an abomination to the Romans and a curse to the Jews. To this day it remains offensive to everyone who thinks he or she is a good person.

Most people have a rather high opinion of themselves. They are impressed with their own moral record. They generally tell the truth. They usually put in an honest day's work. They are always kind to animals. True, they may have a few minor flaws, but by and large they are good people. Their virtues far outweigh their vices. Certainly they are good enough to get into heaven. They are not saints perhaps, but one way or another they will be able to squeeze through the pearly gates.

What is offensive about the cross is that it utterly contradicts this line of reasoning. Consider what the cross says. It says you are *not righteous*. It says you are a sinner. It says you do not measure up to God's perfect standard. The reason it was necessary for Jesus to be crucified was because of the sins of humanity, your own sins included.

The cross also says you are *helpless*. It says you cannot get into heaven on the strength of your own record. You need someone else to offer his perfect life on your behalf. This is one difference between Christianity and every other religion. Every other religion tells you to present to God the best record you can. Christianity teaches that God offers his perfect record to you. But that means you cannot gain eternal life without his total help. The death of Christ on the cross proves the helplessness of humanity.

Then the cross says you are *hopeless*. The cross of Christ shows that sin deserves the wrath and curse of God. It proves that without Christ, sinners will perish for their sins. Don't you think that if God could have saved you any other way he would have done it? But there was no other way, because every sin deserves a hell of suffering.

Who wants to be told that he or she is helpless, hopeless, and unrighteous? No one does. The very idea is offensive. Most people are convinced of their own basic goodness. They go through life helping themselves and hoping for the best. These attitudes make the cross offensive to the moral individual. The cross is a warning that you are dead in your sins. It announces that you cannot help yourself, indeed that you are without hope.

JESUS SCORNED THE CROSS

You are helpless, hopeless, and unrighteous—unless, that is, you come to the cross to ask for the help, the hope, and the righteousness of Jesus Christ. Then the cross is full of the hope and help you need.

Jesus is the one person who did not find the cross offensive. He was not disgraced by its disgrace. So the Bible encourages us to "fix our eyes on Jesus . . . who . . . endured the cross, scorning its shame, and sat down at the right hand of the throne of God" (Heb. 12:2).

Jesus scorned the shame of the cross. He had heard that it was an abomination to the Romans. He knew that it was a curse to the Jews, and even to God the Father. He recognized that it was an affront to everyone who wants to get to heaven on his or her own merits. Yet, however offensive the cross may be to others, Jesus Christ scorns its shame and allows it to fall upon himself for our eternal benefit, not allowing that shame to make him turn back from accomplishing the atonement.

This explains the remarkable fact that the cross has survived at all. How could such an offensive emblem persist through the centuries? How could a symbol that was scorned by the Romans, cursed by the Jews, and dismissed by every moral individual endure from one millennium to the next?

Only because the cross was no offense to Jesus Christ. For him, it was the price he gladly paid to save his people. And for everyone who loves him, the cross ceases to be an offense. It becomes instead the proof of the undying love of the Savior who gave his life for them.

. . . making peace

through his blood,

shed on the cross.

COLOSSIANS 1:20

17

THE PEACE OF THE CROSS

Philip Graham Ryken

t is not easy to make peace on earth, and once peace has been made, it is even harder to keep. Neville Chamberlain (1869-1940) learned these lessons the hard way at the outset of World War II. In September 1938, when Chamberlain served as Prime Minister of England, he signed the Munich Agreement with Adolf Hitler. Upon his return to England, he proudly announced that he had achieved "peace in our time."

Six months later Hitler invaded Poland, and the world was pulled into the abyss of war. Neville Chamberlain proved to be a prophet like those Jeremiah warned about in the Old Testament: "'Peace, peace,' they say, when there is no peace" (Jer. 8:11).

Rumors of peace continue to be whispered at the present time. From time to time peace is announced in the Balkans, Northern Ireland, the Middle East, or elsewhere. The world leaders sign their treaties. The media gather. The crowds cheer. Yet there is no peace. In fact, politicians no longer speak of "peace," but only of a "peace process." As far as anyone can tell, it is all process and very little peace.

AT WAR WITH GOD

There is a reason the world seems always to be at war. It is because humanity is in rebellion against God. Ever since the day Adam and

Eve ate the forbidden fruit, there has been an unceasing war between man and God. The hostilities began with the sin of our first parents, and they soon escalated.

> *Then the eyes of both of them were opened, and they realized they were naked; so they sewed fig leaves together and made coverings for themselves. Then the man and his wife heard the sound of the LORD God as he was walking in the garden in the cool of the day, and they hid from the Lord God among the trees of the garden. But the Lord God called to the man, "Where are you?" He answered, "I heard you in the garden, and I was afraid because I was naked; so I hid."*
>
> *—Gen. 3:7-10*

Camouflage and retreat! These are the strategems of war. Adam and Eve knew that a breach had come between themselves and God. The sound of God's footstep, which once they had greeted with joy, now filled them with dread. By trying to cover up and hide, our first parents were drawing the battle lines.

Every human being is a son of Adam or a daughter of Eve. Therefore, everyone enters this world already at war with God. This is true of any child born in wartime. The child's allegiance already has been determined. He or she has chosen sides, or perhaps had them chosen. In the same way, every human born into this world is prepared to take up arms against God.

How can we tell we are at war with God? First, there is the testimony of God's Word, which says we are "alienated from God and enemies in [our] minds because of [our] evil behavior" (Col. 1:21). We love everything the world has to offer, but "friendship with the world is hatred toward God" (Jas. 4:4). We know we are "God's enemies" because the Bible tells us so (Rom. 5:10).

Then there is the evidence of a troubled conscience. Do you ever feel guilty for something you think, say, or do? Do you ever get angry unjustly? Do you ever say anything untrue? Do you ever take anything that does not belong to you? Most people have guilty consciences. They would rather not have God know where they have been, what they have been doing, or what they have been thinking. The guilty conscience is an alarm of war. It testifies that our sin has made us enemies of God.

Another way to tell that we do not have peace with God is that we are not at peace with one another. Divorce is on the rise. Child abuse is rampant. The legal system is overwhelmed with a backlog of lawsuits and countersuits. To say nothing of long-standing feuds between neighbors or petty gossip in the workplace. If we were at peace with God, there would be peace in our times. But as it is, the whole world is at war.

A Peace Offering

What the world needs is the peace of the cross. The place where the war against heaven comes to an end is at the cross of Christ. "God was pleased . . . through [Jesus] to reconcile to himself all things . . . by making peace through his blood, shed on the cross" (Col. 1:19-20).

One of the terms the Bible uses to describe peace between God and humanity is *reconciliation*. The basic meaning of *reconcile* is to make an exchange.[1] The word was used in biblical times to describe making change in the marketplace. Suppose you hand me a dollar bill. If I give you back two quarters, two dimes, five nickels, and five pennies, we have been reconciled. Trust me, we have made a fair transaction.

When the Bible speaks about reconciliation with God, it means an exchange has taken place. There is a change in our relationship with him. Hatred has been traded in for love. We are no longer God's enemies; now we are his friends.

Reconciliation does not mean that we change our minds about God. Left to ourselves, we never would change our minds about God.

We would continue in perpetual rebellion. Reconciliation never would take place. If men and women are to be reconciled to God, God must take the first step. He has to take the initiative. And he does.

Leon Morris explains that "God is never said in so many words to be reconciled to man. Almost always he is the subject of the verb and is said to reconcile man to Himself. This manner of speaking puts emphasis on the truth that the process of reconciliation origi-nates with God. It is only by the outworking of his love that man can be brought into right relationships with his Maker."[2]

Whenever the Bible speaks about reconciliation, God is always the one who does the reconciling. That is how it is in Colossians 1: "God was . . . pleased to reconcile to himself all things" (vv. 19-20).

Reconciliation teaches something remarkable about the character of God: he befriends his enemies. He loves those who hate him. He offers peace to those who have waged war against him. Although he is the one who has been wronged, he is the one who makes things right. He does all this while the battle still rages. "When we were God's enemies, we were reconciled to him through the death of his Son" (Rom. 5:10).

The way God reconciles us to himself is through the cross of Christ, specifically through the blood of Christ. God made "peace through his blood, shed on the cross" (Col. 1:20). The crucifixion of Jesus Christ was a peace offering. The breach between humanity and God was caused by sin. That sin had to be paid for and removed in order for reconciliation to take place.

Peace never occurs simply by ignoring what started the war in the first place. True reconciliation depends on dealing with the real prob-lem. H. Maldwyn Hughes explains that "there can be no reconciliation between persons by ignoring the deep-seated ground of offence. This must be eradicated and destroyed if the reconciliation is to be com-plete and lasting. If God and man are to be reconciled, it cannot be by the simple expedient of ignoring sin, but only by overcoming it."[3]

That is what Jesus was doing on the cross. He was atoning for, defeating, and overcoming sin so that we could be reconciled to God. The prophet Isaiah put this in a beautiful way: "the punishment that brought us peace was upon him" (Isa. 53:5).

It is striking that when the Bible speaks about the peace of the cross, it uses the past tense. In one way or another Scripture says that Jesus Christ has already reconciled man to God on the cross. This is because the crucifixion is an historical event. Therefore, the reconciliation between man and God is complete. According to the Scottish theologian P. T. Forsyth, "Reconciliation was finished in Christ's death. Paul did not preach a gradual reconciliation. He preached what the old divines used to call the finished work. . . . He preached something done once for all."[4]

Reconciliation has already been accomplished!

All that is true, but the peace of the cross still needs to be received. The sinner is not reconciled to God until he or she actually goes to the cross to be reconciled. It is only by trusting in the finished work of Christ that anyone finds peace with God.

BLESSED ARE THE PEACEMAKERS

Peace with God is not the end of the story, however. Everyone who has peace with God also must live at peace with man. "God . . . reconciled us to himself through Christ and gave us the ministry of reconciliation: that God was reconciling the world to himself in Christ, not counting men's sins against them. And he has committed to us the message of reconciliation" (2 Cor. 5:18-19).

In other words, having peace with God means living at peace with everyone else. Christians must have peaceful relationships with their families, friends, neighbors, and coworkers. Anyone who has an enemy must do what God did for his enemies—namely, take the initiative to make reconciliation. That is not always possible, but the Bible tells Christians to "make every effort to live in peace with all men" (Heb. 12:14). One sign that we are at peace with God is that we are able to make peace with one another.

Once there were two women who were not at peace. They had attended the same church for many years. In fact, they had been the best of friends. Yet one of the women committed a serious offense against the other. As a result of her malice, the other woman was driven away from the church. A close friendship degenerated into bitter animosity. For years they neither saw nor spoke to one another.

Then one day they were reconciled. It happened in the dairy section at the supermarket. The woman who had been wronged bent over to pick up a carton of milk. When she stood up, her adversary was there, with her arms open wide. As they embraced, she apologized for what she had done, and they were reconciled.

The peace between those women flowed from the peace of the cross. Their reconciliation was one small part of what the Bible means when it says that "God was pleased to have all his fullness dwell in [Jesus], and through him to reconcile to himself all things, whether things on earth or things in heaven, by making peace through his blood, shed on the cross" (Col. 1:19-20).

The message of the cross

is foolishness to those

who are perishing,

but to us who are being saved

it is the power of God.

1 CORINTHIANS 1:18

18

THE POWER OF THE CROSS

Philip Graham Ryken

t is hard to imagine anything weaker than a man hanging on a cross. Since he is naked, he is completely vulnerable. He is exposed not only to the elements, but also to the shame of his nakedness. His body is there for all to see in all its frailty.

The weakness of the cross is also physical. The longer the man hangs on the cross, the weaker he becomes. His heart and breath grow faint until he expires. There is nothing he can do to save himself from his inevitable demise. A man crucified is a weakling. He is a victim, not a victor.

The weakness of a crucified man helps explain why so many people have rejected Jesus Christ. They have perhaps heard about his teaching. They know that his biography is contained somewhere in the Bible. They may even believe that he was crucified. But it does not seem to matter. What is so significant about a man hanging on a cross?

THE OLD, FOOLISH CROSS

Christians believe that the crucifixion of Jesus Christ, with his resurrection, was the most important event in the history of the world. For them, the cross of Christ is the source of all hope and comfort.

Yet the same cross that is so attractive to the followers of Christ is exactly what keeps others from coming to him at all.

This was true already in the days of Christ. The Jews were looking for something supernatural. Under Roman occupation, they controlled neither their own economy nor their own destiny. So the Jews "demand[ed] miraculous signs" (1 Cor. 1:22). They expected God to send a king to deliver them from Roman oppression. They were looking for a supernatural deliverance by a mighty warrior. They would not believe in Jesus unless he showed them a miraculous sign.

The Greeks were looking for proof of a different kind. They were the intellectuals of the ancient world. They spent their time talking about nothing but "the latest ideas" (Acts 17:21). When it came to religion, the Greeks were rationalists. They would not believe that Jesus was the Savior of the world until someone proved it to them on the basis of reasoned evidence. The "Greeks look[ed] for wisdom" (1 Cor. 1:22).

These attitudes explain why neither the Jews nor the Greeks had very much interest in Jesus Christ. He was just a man hanging on a cross. Christ crucified was an obstacle to the Jews. The Bible calls this "a stumbling block" (v. 23) that prevented many of them from coming to salvation. What is so miraculous about a man executed like a common criminal? To the Jews, the cross was an obstacle because it was weak.

To the Greeks, the cross was not so much an obstacle as it was foolishness. Where is the wisdom in dying a God-forsaken death? How could the blood of one man atone for the sins of the whole world? The cross was unimpressive to the Greeks because it did not appeal to their superior intellect. Therefore, Christ crucified was "foolishness to Gentiles" (v. 23) as well as "a stumbling block" to Jews.

The cross of Christ remains an obstacle to the modern mind. Many religious people are looking for exactly what people were looking for in the time of Christ. They will not trust in Jesus until God shows them another miracle or gives them a better proof.

Like the ancient Jews, some are waiting for a supernatural sign. This explains the popularity of fortune-tellers and faith healers. For a small fee they will reveal the future or perform a televised miracle. When it comes to Christianity, some people demand a miracle before they will believe in Jesus Christ. "If only God would come down out of heaven and show himself to me, then I would believe him," they say.

Miracle-seekers are like the boy in a short story by John Updike called "Pigeon Feathers":

> Though the experiment frightened him, he lifted his hands high into the darkness above his face and begged Christ to touch them. Not hard or long: the faintest, quickest grip would be final for a lifetime.[1]

Eventually God did touch the boy—but not with physical hands.

Other people are looking for wisdom. Not many perhaps, but at least some. They go to the university. They study philosophy. They read about the latest advances in human science. When it comes to religion, they want God to answer all their questions. They refuse to believe in Jesus Christ until someone can unravel the mysteries of creation, or solve the problem of human freedom, or show them physical evidence for the existence of the soul. They are like the philosopher Bertrand Russell (1872-1970), who could hardly wait to appear before the throne of God to say, "Not enough evidence, God! Not enough evidence!"

The world is still looking for a proof of mind or miracle. But all Christianity offers is a God-man dying on a cross. Crucifixion does not even show up on the radar of postmodern expectations. If God wants to perform some other miracle or provide some other proof, then perhaps the world will listen. But until such time, the old, foolish cross remains an obstacle to faith.

THE POWER OF LOVE

The cross of Christ refuses to meet human expectations. At one level the crucifixion of Jesus is just another Roman execution. It seems weak to those who look for strength. It appears foolish to those who look for wisdom. But this is only when the cross is viewed in human terms.

From God's perspective, the cross is neither impotent nor ignorant. It is full of power and wisdom. "The message of the cross is foolishness to those who are perishing, but to us who are being saved it is the power of God" (1 Cor. 1:18). It helps to remember that God is much wiser and stronger than any human being. God has more intelligence than all the geniuses in the world put together. He has more power in his left pinky, so to speak, than the world's strongest man has in his entire biceps. "For the foolishness of God is wiser than man's wisdom, and the weakness of God is stronger than man's strength" (v. 25).

However weak or foolish it seems to mere mortals, the cross of Christ displays the power and wisdom of God. It does this in several ways. First, it is a powerful demonstration of God's love.

When it comes to love, actions speak louder than words. A man may say that he loves a woman, but how can she know for sure? She will know that he really does love her when he shows her his love. A gift would be nice, especially if the gift is precious or rare. Or if the gift comes at great cost. Or best of all, if the gift is what she has always needed or wanted.

That is exactly the kind of gift God gave when he sent Jesus to die on the cross. It was a precious gift because it was the gift of God's own Son. It was a rare gift because Jesus is God's only Son. It was a costly gift, the costliest of all, because it came at the expense of Jesus' lifeblood. Best of all, the cross of Christ was exactly the gift humanity was hoping for. Jesus died on the cross to effect eternal friendship with God, which is the longing of every human heart. "For God so loved the world that he gave his one and only Son, that whoever believes in him shall not perish but have eternal life" (John 3:16).

The power of the cross is the power of love. When Jesus was crucified, he showed the full extent of God's love. For those who are looking for proof, the cross is proof enough. The crucifixion of Jesus Christ is the only evidence needed to demonstrate God's undying love for sinners.

THE WISDOM OF FORGIVENESS

The cross is also a powerful demonstration of God's wisdom, the wisdom of his forgiveness. Human beings do not approach God on an even footing. They come to him having already accumulated an enormous debt. It is the debt sinners owe to God because of their sin. All the lies they have told, all the curses they have uttered, all the wounds they have inflicted, all the worship they have withheld amounts to an enormous debt of sin. How could such a vast debt ever be settled?

This is where God's wisdom comes in. God did not set up an elaborate payment plan that would take an eternity for sinners to pay off. The entire debt was settled on the cross. God accepted the sacrificial death of his Son as full payment for sin. Jesus paid for each and every last sin when he was crucified. He died on the cross so God could forgive all the sins of all his people all at once.

There is a great deal of wisdom in the cross, therefore, as well as unlimited power. The wisdom and power of the cross is the wisdom and power of sin forgiven. For those who are looking for a miracle, the cross is miracle enough. The crucifixion of Jesus Christ offers forgiveness full and free.

POWER UNTO SALVATION

What do you think of the cross of Christ? Is it wise or foolish? Is it strong or weak? These questions demand an answer. The cross is either one or the other; it cannot be both. If the cross of Christ is the power of God unto salvation, it is the strongest, wisest thing God has ever done. But if the cross has no power to save, then it is irrelevant to modern life. So the question bears repeating: What do you think of the cross of Christ?

Sadly, some people do not understand the cross. Some of them never will. The crucifixion of Jesus Christ will remain foolish to them until the day of judgment. This is because the cross only makes sense to those who are saved by it. "For the message of the cross is foolishness to those who are perishing, but to us who are being saved it is the power of God" (1 Cor. 1:18). To put this another way, the cross only makes sense to those who trust in Jesus Christ for their salvation. For them, the cross is the proof of God's love and the miracle of God's forgiveness. It is neither weak nor foolish, but strong and wise.

What should someone do if the cross still seems foolish? The obvious thing to do is to keep trying to understand it, to ask God what it means. To all who ask for help instead of a miracle or an answer, Jesus Christ gives the love and the forgiveness of the cross. Then they know that the cross of Christ is the power of God.

. . . having disarmed

the powers and authorities,

he made a public spectacle of them,

triumphing over them by the cross.

COLOSSIANS 2:15

19

THE TRIUMPH OF THE CROSS

Philip Graham Ryken

When Jesus Christ was crucified outside Jerusalem, at least three things were nailed to his cross. The first was Jesus himself. As the Bible simply states, "They crucified him" (Mark 15:24).

The Roman custom was to drive heavy iron nails through the wrists and heel bones of the victim. This is what the Roman soldiers did to Jesus; they "put him to death by nailing him to the cross" (Acts 2:23). After he was raised from the dead, Jesus was able to show his disciples the nail prints in his hands (John 20:25-27), because he had been nailed to the cross.

Something else was nailed to the cross where Jesus died. It was the announcement the governor had "prepared and fastened to the cross. It read: 'JESUS OF NAZARETH, THE KING OF THE JEWS'" (John 19:19). That publicity was God's doing. He wanted everyone who witnessed the crucifixion to know that his Son was the true king of Israel. In all likelihood that public notice was fastened to the cross of Christ with a hammer and a nail.

A CERTIFICATE OF DEBT

One more thing was nailed to the cross of Christ. Surprisingly, it was something God nailed to the cross himself, even though it was invisible to the human eye. The Bible says that God "forgave us all our sins, having canceled the written code, with its regulations, that was against us and that stood opposed to us; he took it away, nailing it to the cross" (Col. 2:13-14). The third thing nailed to the cross was a "written code."

What kind of "written code" was it? To answer that question, it helps to know something about business transactions in the Roman world. The Greek word for "written code" (*cheirographon*) means "handwritten" or "signed by hand." It was used to refer to any kind of personal autograph.

The word had a specialized meaning, however. In the world of finance it referred to a certificate of debt signed by the debtor's own hand. The scholar J. B. Lightfoot (1828-1889) called it "a note of hand, a bond or obligation."[1] Today it might be called an I.O.U. A man who owed money carefully wrote out the amount he was obliged to pay back to his creditors. Then he confirmed the grand total of his indebtedness with his signature.

This gives us at least the beginning of an answer to our question. The "written code" God nailed to the cross was a bill of debt. But that raises still more questions. How large was the debt? To whom was it owed? Most important of all, whose autograph was at the bottom of that handwritten note?

The Bible gives enough clues to help answer those questions. What was nailed to the cross was "the written code, with its regulations, that was against us and that stood opposed to us" (Col. 2:14). "Regulations" obviously has something to do with the Law. It calls to mind the rules for life that God first gave to Moses and that are summarized in the Ten Commandments: "You shall have no other gods before me. . . . You shall not murder. You shall not commit adultery. You shall not steal," and so forth (Exod. 20:1-17).

There is nothing wrong with those regulations. God has every right to expect people to live good and holy lives. He has given us his rules for our good. Any society that worships God alone, safeguards life, preserves sex for marriage, and respects private property is a good society. God's Law is not the problem.

The problem is that human beings are lawbreakers. "No mere man since the fall is able in this life perfectly to keep the commandments of God, but doth daily break them in thought, word, and deed" (*Westminster Shorter Catechism*, Answer 82). We worship anything and everything except God. We curse God when things go wrong at the office. We do not give our fathers and mothers the respect they deserve. We stretch the truth, cheat, and steal. Or we are discontent with what we have because we want something else. In one way or another we do not keep God's regulations.

Since we are lawbreakers, God's Law is against us. It is our enemy. It stands opposed to us. The list of God's laws is also a list of our sins. Every one of God's regulations is another reminder that we have sinned against a holy God. So this is the hand-signed bill the Bible has in mind when it speaks of "the written code." It is a record of the infinite debt we owe to God because we have broken his Law.

By now we clearly see what was nailed to the cross of Christ along with Jesus and with the notice of his kingship. It was a bill showing the charges we had run up by breaking God's Law. It was a legal note showing that we owed an infinite debt to God because of our sin. That certificate of debt had our own signature at the bottom. And since "the wages of sin is death" (Rom. 6:23), it was as if we had signed our own death warrant.

THE DEBT CANCELED

The triumph of the cross is that God crucified the certificate of our debt to his Law. He took away "the written code, with its regulations, that was against us and that stood opposed to us. . . nailing it to the cross" (Col. 2:14).

When that I.O.U. was nailed to the cross with Christ, all our sins were forgiven. Our debt was cleared. As the Bible puts it, God "canceled the written code." In the Greek original, the word "canceled" means "to blot out" or "to wipe away." The idea is that the debt we once owed to God because of our sin has been completely erased.

This is the triumph of the cross. God canceled the entire debt of our sin by nailing it to the cross. He forgave all our sins when Jesus died on the cross. Since each and every one of our sins was nailed to the cross with Christ, the entire amount of our debt has been cleared. There are no outstanding charges.

There is a beautiful verse about the triumph of the cross over sin in a famous hymn by Horatio G. Spafford. The events of Spafford's life were tragic. In November 1873 he sent his wife and four daughters to Europe on board the French liner *Ville du Havre*. During the Atlantic passage, the steamer collided with another ship, and most of the passengers were lost at sea. Among them were Spafford's daughters, although his wife was rescued.

Spafford booked passage on the next available ship. Just as the vessel neared the spot where his daughters had drowned, Spafford wrote the hymn "It Is Well with My Soul." Even in grief he was able to take comfort in the triumph of the cross.

> *My sin—O the bliss of this glorious thought!—*
> *My sin, not in part, but the whole,*
> *Is nailed to the cross and I bear it no more;*
> *Praise the Lord, praise the Lord, O my soul!*

Spafford was remembering the second chapter of Colossians, for that is the place where the Bible says God forgave the whole of our sin by nailing it to the cross.[2]

A PUBLIC SPECTACLE

In the cross of Christ, God not only triumphed over sin, he also triumphed over Satan. Satan was such an old enemy, and the cross was such a great triumph, that God could not keep this victory to himself. After explaining how God nailed our sins to the cross, the Bible goes on to say that "having disarmed the powers and authorities, he made a public spectacle of them, triumphing over them by the cross" (v. 15).

Here again it helps to know something about ancient Roman culture. When a general returned home after winning a great war victory, he led a public procession through the streets of Rome. Following in his train were the prisoners he had seized in battle. The general made a public spectacle of his captives because the prisoners of war were the proof of total victory.

God did the same thing to Satan on the cross. Satan had been waging war against God for centuries. The earthly battle between heaven and hell was first joined in the Garden of Eden, where Satan tempted Eve to commit the first sin. Ever since, Satan has tried to destroy God's people by leading them further into sin. He watched with uncontained glee as human beings fell more and more helplessly into debt. He knew that they would never be able to pay what they owed to God for breaking his Law.

But there was one thing that Satan forgot to include in his calculations. He did not count on the triumph of the cross. He did not know that Jesus Christ would pay the full price for sin by dying on the cross. He could not see that when Jesus was crucified, the infinite debt we owe to God would be nailed there with him. By the time Satan realized that the cross was the triumph of God rather than the death of God, it was too late.

The Bible says that when God nailed our sins to the cross, he "disarmed the powers and authorities" (v. 15). "Powers and authorities" refers to Satan and his demons. For a time God allowed them to hold the power of sin and the authority of death over God's people. But their power and authority were neutralized on the cross. The Puritan Matthew Henry (1662-1714) put it like this: "The devil and all the powers of hell were conquered and disarmed by the dying

Redeemer."[3] When Christ died on the cross, the enemies of God lost the power of sin and the authority of death.

Thus the crucifixion of Jesus Christ was an exhibition of God's victory over Satan. "Having disarmed the powers and authorities, he made a public spectacle of them, triumphing over them by the cross" (v. 15). Like a mighty general, God conquered the devil and all his demons through the cross. Then he put them on public display. The cross was God's victory parade. It showed that God had triumphed over sin and over Satan by nailing our debts to the cross.

The cross is God's triumph. It is also a triumph for everyone who trusts in Jesus Christ for salvation. The Reverend Ed King explained the triumph of the cross when he preached at the funeral of James Chaney, an African-American peace worker murdered by the Ku Klux Klan in August 1964. King knew that the Klan uses its cross for evil purposes, but he wanted to reclaim the triumphant cross of Christ. "The cross is not a burned cross," he preached. "It is the one cross of Calvary that is stained with the blood of Jesus, God's Son. God gave his Son for all of us and this is the cross that we follow— the cross that means victory."

May I never boast

except in the cross

of our Lord

Jesus Christ.

GALATIANS 6:14

20

THE BOAST OF THE CROSS

Philip Graham Ryken

here is something curious about boasting. Despite the fact that nobody likes a braggart, everybody brags anyway. People boast about anything and everything—their grandchildren, their bank accounts, their waistlines, their bowling averages, their travel plans, their accomplishments, sometimes even their indiscretions.

Recently a most outlandish boast appeared on television. Commercials involve a fair amount of bragging anyway, but this one reached a new low in advertising. An automobile company proudly announced its "most impressive safety advance ever . . . a car that can save your soul."

GOD FORBID!

The apostle Paul never would have boasted about an automobile. Or anything else, for that matter. "May I never boast," he wrote to the Galatians (Gal. 6:14). "Far be it from me to make a boast." Or more literally, "God forbid that I should ever boast!"

Since Paul was a scholar of the Old Testament, he knew that the Bible forbids boasting. "This is what the LORD says," according to the prophet Jeremiah: "Let not the wise man boast of his wisdom or the strong man boast of his strength or the rich man boast of his riches"

(Jer. 9:23). If a man cannot boast about his brainpower, his muscle power, or his buying power, what can he boast about? Nothing at all. King Solomon wisely gave this warning: "Let another praise you, and not your own mouth; someone else, and not your own lips" (Prov. 27:2). In other words, let someone else blow your horn.

Boasting is never attractive. The worst kind of all is bragging about one's religious accomplishments. Yet that is exactly what some people were doing in the days of Paul. Many of the first Christians were Jews by birth, so they had been circumcised in their infancy. Circumcision was the Old Testament sign of belonging to God's people. If a Gentile wanted to join the Jewish community, he had to be circumcised. Some early Christians thought that circumcision was still a requirement for salvation. Anyone who wants to become a true follower of Jesus Christ, they said, also has to get circumcised in the Old Testament fashion.

It seems strange to modern ears, but the pro-circumcision people were so proud of being circumcised that they started bragging about it. The more Gentiles they could persuade to get circumcised, the more they bragged. This is what the Bible says about them: "They want you to be circumcised that they may boast about your flesh" (Gal. 6:13). Talk about being holier than thou!

Religious people do not brag about circumcision the way they once did, but they still find plenty of things to boast about. They brag about their church attendance. Or their converts. Or their style of worship. Or their devotional habits. Or their political commitments. Or their particular brand of theology. In one way or another they find subtle ways to call attention to how spiritual they are. One of the main reasons some people are so hostile toward the church is that Christians can be so smug.

Paul himself had plenty of religious things to boast about. On one occasion he listed the highlights of his spiritual résumé: "Circumcised on the eighth day, of the people of Israel, of the tribe of Benjamin, a Hebrew of Hebrews; in regard to the law, a Pharisee; as for zeal, persecuting the church; as for legalistic righteousness, faultless" (Phil. 3:5-6). What more could anyone ask for? Paul had all the right connections. He came from a good family, attended the best schools, and believed the most orthodox theology.

The man had as much to boast about as anyone else, if he had wanted to. But when Paul came to know Jesus Christ, he realized that he had nothing to boast about. All his religious accomplishments were a load of rubbish (Phil. 3:8). God forbid that he should boast about any of them.

A MOST UNUSUAL OBSESSION

There is only one thing in all the universe worth boasting about. The Bible allows for a single exception: "May I never boast except in the cross of our Lord Jesus Christ" (Gal. 6:14).

The surprising thing about this boast is that in the ancient world crucifixion was nothing to boast about. In an earlier chapter we noted that the cross was an offense to the Romans and a curse to the Jews. The New Testament scholar F. F. Bruce concludes that the

> object of Paul's present boasting was, by all ordinary standards of his day, the most ignoble of all objects—a matter of unrelieved shame, not of boasting. It is difficult, after sixteen centuries and more during which the cross has been a sacred symbol, to realize the unspeakable horror and loathing which the very mention or thought of the cross provoked in Paul's day. The word *crux* was unmentionable in polite Roman society (Cicero, *Pro Rabirio* 16); even when one was being condemned to death by crucifixion the sentence used an archaic formula which served as a sort of euphemism: *arbori infelici suspendito*, "hang him on the unlucky tree" (Cicero, ibid. 13). In the eastern provinces of the empire the Greek word *stauros* ("cross") must have inspired comparable dread and disgust to its Latin equivalent.[1]

Thus it was shocking for Paul even to mention the cross, let alone boast about it. If anything, one would expect the first Christians to deny that Jesus died on the cross. Or at most, if they were honest, to admit this fact only with the greatest reluctance.

Far from being reluctant, however, Paul was eager to boast about the cross. As John Stott explains, "That which the average Roman citizen regarded as an object of shame, disgrace and even disgust was for Paul his pride, boasting and glory."[2] Indeed, the English word "boast" is not strong enough to express his attitude about the cross. "There is no exact equivalent in the English language to *kauchaomai*. It means to boast in, glory in, trust in, rejoice in, revel in, live for. The object of our boast or 'glory' fills our horizons, engrosses our attention, and absorbs our time and energy. In a word, our 'glory' is our obsession."[3]

DEAD TO SIN, ALIVE TO GOD'S LOVE

Why are Christians so obsessed with the cross? Why do they revel in it? What makes it something to boast about?

First, the cross means the death of sin. Paul's full statement runs as follows: "May I never boast except in the cross of our Lord Jesus Christ, through which the world has been crucified to me, and I to the world" (v. 14). By "the world" is meant the world without God, in all its vanity. The world represents the tyranny of sin over humanity. Every human being is born in sin and continues to sin. Even Paul himself was in bondage to sin. He was enslaved to the world, with all its wicked ways.

The crucifixion of Jesus Christ, however, struck a mortal blow to sin's worldly power. As we saw in our last study, it was as if sin was nailed to the cross with Jesus (Col. 2:13-15). He died on the cross not only to atone for sin, but ultimately to bring it to an end.

Christians boast in the cross because it means the beginning of the end of their sin. Sin no longer holds them in its death-grip. More

and more, they are becoming dead to the temptations and entice-
ments of sin. One day, when Christ returns, they will be done with
it once and for all.

Another reason to boast about the cross of Christ is because it is
the greatest demonstration of God's love. It shows the love of God
the Father, who gave up his only Son as a sacrifice to save his people. Therefore, to glory in the cross is to glory in God's love.

A father's love is always something to boast about. This is true at
the human level. A father once put a note in his son's lunch box. It
was just a simple note saying, "Hope you have a nice day at school.
See you when I get home. Love, Dad."

When the boy returned home from school, his mother noticed that
the note was still tucked into his lunch box, unopened. Apparently
the boy hadn't noticed it, so she pulled it out and handed it to him.
He took the note, read it, and began to cry. When his mother hugged
him and asked what was the matter, he said, "I didn't realize Dad loved
me that much."[4] Such is the power of a father's love.

A father's love is all the more powerful when it is divine. The cross
of Christ shows the children of God how deeply they are loved by
their Father in heaven. Boasting about that cross is a way of saying,
"See, my Heavenly Daddy loves me!"

Incidentally, the boast of the cross is not an exclusive boast.
Usually what makes boasting so unpleasant is that the boaster has
something to boast about and you don't. But the boast of the cross
is not intended to keep people on the outside. Anyone may come to
the cross. Jesus invites everyone to come to him, to have sins forgiven, and to receive his eternal love. Boasting in his cross is open
to anyone who will receive him.

THE WONDROUS CROSS

One of the best hymns of the church is based on the words we have
been studying: "May I never boast except in the cross of our Lord

Jesus Christ, through which the world has been crucified to me, and I to the world" (v. 14). The hymn is called "When I Survey the Wondrous Cross." It was written by Isaac Watts (1674-1748), and it is a boast about the only thing in all the world worth boasting about. It rules out all other forms of boasting as God-forbidden. It speaks of the love that flowed from the cross along with the blood of Christ. Finally, it ends with a prayer of commitment to Christ. Make that commitment your own.

> When I survey the wondrous cross
> On which the Prince of glory died,
> My richest gain I count but loss,
> And pour contempt on all my pride.
>
> Forbid it, Lord, that I should boast,
> Save in the death of Christ, my God;
> All the vain things that charm me most—
> I sacrifice them to His blood.
>
> See from His head, His hands, His feet,
> Sorrow and love flow mingled down;
> Did e'er such love and sorrow meet,
> Or thorns compose so rich a crown?
>
> His dying crimson, like a robe,
> Spreads o'er His body on the tree;
> Then am I dead to all the globe,
> And all the globe is dead to me.
>
> Were the whole realm of nature mine,
> That were a present far too small;
> Love so amazing, so divine,
> Demands my soul, my life, my all.

"*If anyone*

would come after me,

he must deny himself

and take up his cross daily

and follow me."

LUKE 9:23

21

THE WAY OF THE CROSS

James Montgomery Boice

he way of the cross is about Christian discipleship, and the problem is that there is very little actual following of Jesus Christ in our time. Discipleship means forsaking everything in order to follow Christ. But for many of today's Christians it is the case that while there is much talk about Christ and even much furious activity that is supposedly done in his name, there is actually very little following of Christ himself. That means there is very little genuine Christianity.

THE LACK OF TRUE DISCIPLESHIP

In Jesus' great sermon on the Mount of Olives uttered shortly before his crucifixion (Matthew 25), the Lord compared professing but unconverted Christians to women waiting for a bridegroom to appear for a wedding banquet. They were waiting faithfully and cried out fervently to him, but they were unprepared for his coming and were shut out of the wedding. They were not saved. Again, Jesus compared those who only profess to be Christians to a man who was given a talent to invest but who failed to use it and was condemned by his master on the day of reckoning. Jesus said that he was thrown "into the darkness, where there will be weeping and gnashing of teeth" (v. 30). In a third comparison he described these people as failing to feed the hungry, give drink to those who were thirsting, receive strangers, clothe the naked, care for the sick, and visit those who were imprisoned. These apparent Christians called Jesus "Lord." They considered themselves to be genuinely converted persons. But they were not Christians and perished utterly.

1. *Defective theology.* There are several reasons why a lack of true discipleship is common in today's church, and the first is a defective theology. This theology separates faith from discipleship and grace from obedience. It teaches that Jesus can be received as one's Savior without his being received as one's Lord. It eliminates the cross.

This defect is common in easy times. In times of persecution those who are becoming Christians count the cost carefully before taking up Christ's cross. Preachers do not beguile them with false promises of an easy life or with the indulgence of their sins. But in easy times the cost does not seem to be so high, and people take the name of "Christ" without undergoing the radical transformation that a true conversion implies. In times like these preachers often delude them with an easy faith in order to increase the numbers on their church rolls, whether or not such people are regenerate.

Dietrich Bonhoeffer called this erroneous theology "cheap grace," saying, "Cheap grace is the preaching of forgiveness without requiring repentance, baptism without church discipline, communion without confession, absolution without personal confession. Cheap grace is grace without discipleship, grace without the cross, grace without Jesus Christ living and incarnate."[1]

Another writer who saw the sad state of contemporary Christianity and bemoaned it was the pastor and devotional author A. W. Tozer. Tozer wrote about the state of the faith in his day, saying, "The whole transaction of religious conversion has been made mechanical and spiritless. Faith may now be exercised without a jar to the moral life and without embarrassment to the Adamic ego. Christ may be 'received' without creating any special love for him in the soul of the receiver. The man is 'saved,' but he is not hungry or thirsty after God. In fact he is specifically taught to be satisfied and encouraged to be content with little."[2]

2. *Lack of self-examination.* It is not only a false theology that has encouraged this fatal lack of discipleship, however. To limit it to that is to excuse ourselves by blaming theologians. This defect also arises from the absence of what the older writers called the "self-examined life."

Most westerners live in a tragically mindless environment. Life is too fast for any serious reflection. Even in the church we are far more often encouraged to join this committee, back that project, or serve on some board than we are counseled to examine our relationship to God and his Son Jesus Christ. So long as we are performing for the church, few will question whether our profession is genuine or spurious. How many sermons suggest that members of a church may not actually be saved, although they are members? Or that a personal, self-denying, costly, and persistent following of Christ is necessary if a person is to be acknowledged by Jesus at the final day? They don't, and the result is that many people drift on in sad self-delusion.

SAYING NO TO SELF

One of the most important things to be said about Christ's definition of discipleship in Luke 9:23 is that the elements he mentions cannot be divorced from each other, even less made progressive steps in the Christian life.

That should be obvious from the way Christ states his demand. If he had intended a progression, at the very least we would have expected him to put "follow me" first, then the matter of self-denial, and perhaps lastly the matter of taking up his cross. But that is not what Jesus is doing. He is spelling out everything that being his disciple entails: 1) self-denial, 2) taking up the cross, and 3) following—all three. Moreover, as the next verses show, if a person rejects those elements of discipleship, he may be trying to "save his life" and "gain the whole world," but the result will be the losing of his very self. He will be rejected by Christ when he returns in glory with his holy angels.

It is evident why this must be true as soon as we think about these terms. When we think about what it means to deny oneself, we are at once brought to the radical distinction between a God-oriented life and a life of unrepentant, self-seeking or sin.

Self-seeking is the opposite of self-denial, and the problem with self-seeking is that it has been the essence of sin from the beginning. It is what caused the fall of Satan. Satan said, "I want my way, and that means that I am going to displace God. I will rule the universe." The key passage that expresses Satan's thoughts is Isaiah 14:13-14, where Satan cried "I will" five times:

> "I will ascend to heaven;
> I will raise my throne above the stars of God;
> I will sit enthroned on the mount of assembly,
>   on the utmost heights of the sacred mountain.
> I will ascend above the tops of the clouds;
> I will make myself like the Most High."

But those verses also explain that Satan will actually be brought low, "to the depths of the pit" (v. 15).

By contrast Jesus said, "I will humble myself in self-denial. I will abase myself in order that others, those the Father has given me and whom I love, might be lifted from sin to glory." As a result of this attitude, God promised that Jesus Christ would be exalted. He would be given the name that is above every name, so that "every tongue [would] confess that Jesus is Lord" (Phil. 2:11).

SAYING YES TO GOD

But it is not only that we are to say no to self, which is what denying self is all about. We are also to say yes to God. Some speak of cross-bearing as if it means enduring the inevitable, but that is not it at all. There are all kinds of things that cannot be avoided—a physical handicap, a deficient academic background, a drunken husband, a profligate wife. These are not crosses. Real crosses involve the surrender of the will. They mean saying yes to some important thing for Jesus' sake.

Cross-bearing involves *prayer and Bible study*. These necessary means of grace take time and must be voluntarily chosen and pursued, rather than other pastimes that we might humanly prefer.

Cross-bearing also involves the items Jesus listed in Matthew 25:31-46—*feeding the hungry, giving drink to the thirsty, receiving the stranger, clothing the naked, caring for the sick, and visiting the one who is in prison*. These things involve denying oneself time, money, and convenience, even when our efforts seem utterly fruitless because the gifts are abused and the one giving them is slighted even by the one he helps. Yet we are to live like this anyway since doing so is saying yes to Jesus.

Taking up our cross also involves *witnessing*. It means putting oneself out for the sake of someone else who needs to hear the Gospel.

Essentially, taking up our cross means *accepting whatever God has given us or made us* and then offering it back to him as "our reasonable service" (Rom. 12:1, KJV). That phrase describes us as priests making sacrifices that are pleasing to God. Priests offer what they have first received. They take the gifts of the worshiper and then offer them up. You and I are in that position. The gifts we receive are from God. We take these gifts—whatever they may be—and then offer them up to God with thanksgiving.

KEEPING OUR EYES ON JESUS

There is only one purpose for a cross, and that is to put the crucified person to death. Death on a cross is a slow death, but it is a certain one, and there is no escaping that for Christ's true followers.

Dietrich Bonhoeffer, who died for his commitment to Christ, understood this principle. He wrote, "When Christ calls a man, he bids him come and die."[3]

But if that is what "the way of the cross" means, why should anyone take up his or her cross and do it? Or even if a person might want to do it, how can he or she ever hope to stay on that hard path? The only thing that will ever get us moving along this path of self-denial and discipleship is fixing our eyes on Jesus and what he has done for us, coming to love him as a result, and thus wanting also to be with him both now and always. Jesus is our only possible model for self-denial. He is the very image of cross-bearing. And it is for love of him and a desire to be like him that we take up our cross and willingly follow him.

Seeing this was the turning point in the life of Count Zinzendorf, the founder of the Moravian fellowships. In a little chapel near his estates in Europe there was a remarkable picture of Jesus Christ. The artist was a true child of God, and he had painted love for Christ and the love of Christ into his portrait as few have done before or since. Underneath it were the lines: "All this I did for thee; what hast thou done for me?"

One day Zinzendorf entered the chapel and was arrested by the portrait. He recognized the love of Christ that had been painted into the face of the Master. He saw the pierced hands, the bleeding forehead, the wounded side. He read the couplet: "All this I did for thee; what hast thou done for me?" Gradually a new revelation of the claim of Christ upon his life came on him. He was unable to move. Hours passed. As the day waned, the lingering rays of sunlight fell upon the bowed form of the young nobleman, now weeping out his devotion to him whose love had conquered his heart.

That is what moves a person to follow after Jesus in the path of self-denial. It is what moves one to be a Christian in the first place—

—not the promise of rewards, though there are rewards, nor an escape from hell, though following after Christ does mean deliverance from hell's terrors. What moves one to be a Christian is the love of Jesus, for the sake of which he endured the cross. Those who have been won by that love will not allow anything to keep them from continuing on that way.

N O T E S

Chapter 1: The Heart of God

1. Cicero, *The Verrine Orations*, trans, L. H. G. Greenwood, *Loeb Classical Library* (Cambridge, Mass.: Harvard University Press, 1953), vol. 2, p. 170.

2. John Charles Ryle, *Expository Thoughts on the Gospels: St. Luke* (Cambridge, England: James Clarke & Co., 1976), vol. 2, p. 463.

Chapter 3: Family Ties

1. Robertson McQuilkin, "Muriel's Blessing," *Christianity Today*, February 5, 1996, p. 32.

2. William Barclay, *The Gospel of John*, rev. ed. (Philadelphia: The Westminster Press, 1975), vol. 2, p. 257.

3. Thomas Warton the Elder, "Ode on the Passion," in Robert Atwan and Lawrence Wieder, eds., *Chapters into Verse: Poetry in English Inspired by the Bible* (New York: Oxford University Press, 1993), vol. 2, pp. 214-215.

Chapter 4: Human After All

1. Matthew Henry, *Commentary on the Whole Bible*, vol. 5, *Matthew to John* (New York: Fleming H. Revell, n.d.), p. 1200.

Chapter 5: Forsaken, Yet Not Forsaken

1. Jonathan Kozol, *Rachel and Her Children: Homeless Families in America* (New York: Crown, 1988), pp. 67, 69.

2. J. Blinzler, *The Trial of Jesus* (Westminster, Md.: Newman, 1959), p. 261.

Chapter 6: Mission Accomplished

1. Charles Haddon Spurgeon, "Christ's Dying Word for His Church," in *Sermons on the Gospel of John* (Grand Rapids, Mich.: Zondervan, 1966), p. 170.

2. Thomas Boston, *Human Nature in Its Fourfold State* (Edinburgh: Banner of Truth, 1964), p. 331.

Chapter 7: Homeward Bound

1. Charles Haddon Spurgeon, "The Last Words of Christ on the Cross," *Metropolitan Tabernacle Pulpit*, vol. 45 (Pasadena, Tex.: Pilgrim Publications, 1977), p. 502.

Chapter 8: A Word for the Seeker

1. Margaret Hannay, "Mary Magdalene," *A Dictionary of Biblical Tradition in English Literature*, ed. David Lyle Jeffrey (Grand Rapids, Mich.: Eerdmans, 1992), pp. 486-489.

2. Cited in James Montgomery Boice, *The Gospel of John: An Expositional Commentary* (Grand Rapids, Mich.: Zondervan, 1979), vol. 5, pp. 281-282.

3. "Rosh Ha-Shanah," 1:8, *The Mishnah,* trans. Herbert Danby (London: Oxford, 1933), p. 189.

Chapter 9: A Word for the Fearful

1. Madeleine L'Engle, *The Glorious Impossible* (New York: Simon & Schuster, 1990), preface.

2. Bertrand Russell, *Why I Am Not a Christian* (New York: Simon & Schuster, 1957).

Chapter 10: A Word for the Restless

1. Don Richardson, *Peace Child* (Glendale, Calif.: G/L Publications, 1974), pp. 154-155.

Chapter 12: A Word for the Skeptical

1. See Gershom Scholem, *Sabbatai Sevi: The Mystical Messiah, 1626-1676* (Princeton, N.J.: Princeton University Press, 1973), p. 679.

2. Charles Hodge, *A Commentary on the First Epistle to the Corinthians* (London: Banner of Truth, 1964), p. 314.

Chapter 14: A Word for Everyone

1. John R. W. Stott, "The Great Commission," in *One Race, One Gospel, One Task: World Congress on Evangelism, Berlin 1966, Official Reference Volumes*, eds. Carl F. H. Henry and W. Stanley Mooneyham (Minneapolis: World Wide Publications, 1966), vol. 1, p. 46.

Chapter 15: The Necessity of the Cross

1. George Lindbeck, "Justification and Atonement: An Ecumenical Trajectory," unpublished paper, pp. 45-46.

2. See Owen's profound work *The Death of Death in the Death of Christ* (Edinburgh: Banner of Truth, 1959).

3. Emil Brunner, *The Mediator*, trans. Olive Wyon (1927; reprint, Philadelphia: Westminster, 1947), pp. 450, 470.

Chapter 16: The Offense of the Cross

1. Origen, Commentary on Matthew 27:22ff., in F. F. Bruce, *The Epistle to the Hebrews*, New International Commentary on the New Testament (Grand Rapids, Mich.: Eerdmans, 1990), p. 338.

2. Cicero, *In Verrem*, II, 5, 165, in John Stott, *The Cross of Christ* (Downers Grove, IL: InterVarsity, 1986), p. 24.

3. Bruce, *The Epistle to the Hebrews*, p. 338.

4. Cicero, *In Verrem*, II, 5, 170, in Stott, *The Cross of Christ*, p. 24.

5. Cicero, *Pro Rabirio*, 5, in Bruce, *The Epistle to the Hebrews*, p. 338.

6. Stott, *The Cross of Christ*, p. 25.

7. Justin Martyr, *Dialogue with Trypho, a Jew*, ch. 89, eds. Alexander Roberts and James Donaldson, *Ante-Nicene Fathers* (New York, 1885; reprint, Peabody, Mass: Hendrickson, 1994), vol. 1, p. 244.

Chapter 17: The Peace of the Cross

1. Leon Morris, *The Apostolic Preaching of the Cross* (London, 1965; reprint, Grand Rapids, Mich.: Eerdmans, 1994), p. 215.

2. Ibid., p. 220.

3. H. Maldwyn Hughes, *What Is the Atonement?* (London: n.p., n.d.), p. 146.

4. P. T. Forsyth, *The Work of Christ* (London: n.p., 1948), p. 86.

Chapter 18: The Power of the Cross

1. John Updike, *Pigeon Feathers and Other Stories* (New York: Knopf, 1962).

Chapter 19: The Triumph of the Cross

1. J. B. Lightfoot, *St. Paul's Epistles to the Colossians and to Philemon*

(London, 1875; reprint, Lynn, Mass.: Hendrickson, 1981), p. 187.

2. Lindsay L. Terry, *Devotionals from Famous Hymn Stories* (Grand Rapids, Mich.: Baker, 1986), pp. 11-12.

3. Matthew Henry, *Matthew Henry's Commentary on the Whole Bible*, 6 vols. (New York: Revell, n.d.), vol. 6, n.p.

Chapter 20: The Boast of the Cross

1. F. F. Bruce, *The Epistle to the Galatians: A Commentary on the Greek Text*, New International Greek Testament Commentary (Grand Rapids, Mich.: Eerdmans, 1982), p. 271.

2. John R. W. Stott, *The Cross of Christ* (Downers Grove, Ill.: InterVarsity, 1986), p. 349.

3. Ibid., p. 349.

4. Recounted in Gary and Anne Marie Ezzo, *Growing Kids God's Way: Biblical Ethics for Parenting* (Chatsworth, Calif.: Growing Families International, 1993), pp. 95-96.

Chapter 21: The Way of the Cross

1. Dietrich Bonhoeffer, *The Cost of Discipleship* (New York: Macmillan, 1966), p. 47. Original German edition 1937.

2. A. W. Tozer, *The Pursuit of God* (Harrisburg, Penn.: Christian Publications, 1948), pp. 12-13.

3. Bonhoeffer, *The Cost of Discipleship*, p. 99.